'THE ... YOURS!'

DEDICATION

To Don Mclean

'THE JOB'S YOURS!'

John Waddingham BA (Hons)

RIGHT WAY

CONTENTS

PART ONE

INTRODUCTION

So You're Looking For A Job
This book is written for those people who seek employment, either because they are currently out of work, or because they wish to improve on their present post. The book is necessary, I believe, because high unemployment today places great demands upon the job hunter. The changes in the British economy, plus new developments in technology and production, distribution and administration, have resulted in a complete change in recruitment and allocation of human resources.

In the course of my work as a Job Club leader and Redundancy Counsellor, I have dealt with people from many different walks of life who were trying to re-enter employment. I have also worked with individuals who wished to change their direction, and who sought my advice and help. Despite high unemployment I have helped hundreds of people return to work. I have successfully remotivated people who had lost confidence and who honestly thought that they would never work again.

I have achieved personal satisfaction from my work, and the confidence that my experience and abilities in job search are second to none.

One example of my achievements is David, aged 45 years. He had always worked in the engineering industry and, having been made redundant, felt that his useful working life was over. Despite his initial pessimistic view he had patience enough to listen to my advice, and to follow it up. We identified other areas of work to which he could transfer with the minimum of training, and then he began his applications. The fact that he had never before written a letter of application or sat an interview was typical of many of my clients. I explained that anyone can make good applications, regardless of their background or absence from the job market.

Within five weeks he had achieved two interviews, an event he had never managed before in two years of unemployment! He got a job on the seventh week of his Job Club membership, as a warehouse operative, and is still working happily with his new employer.

June, aged 38, is another good example. Having brought up her children and looking after the house, she felt that she was unemployable. She thought that because new technology had developed in office work since her last job, she would be unable to cope with clerical work, and that employers were passing her over for younger, more skilled, candidates.

The first thing I did when I met June was to identify her skills, and then investigate courses to re-train her, equipping her with up-to-date office skills. I also looked over her applications, and found that she was still using old fashioned, long-winded letters, rather than a short letter and a CV. We put together a CV and enrolled her on a part-time course for office skills and WP operation. We also arranged volunteer work with a local charity who wanted an office worker for five hours per week. This gave her practice in an office environment, helped to build her confidence, and added to her CV.

Result? Within ten weeks she had gained a job with a large insurance company, on the strength of her experience and her new skills. Afterwards she told me that she had almost given up applying for clerical work and was about to start looking at jobs in other areas, feeling that her situation was hopeless. She admitted that she would not have thought of volunteer work and part-time education without attending my course, and that both these ideas had helped her out of the rut into which she had settled.

Both the above examples are typical of the cases I have handled over the last three years. My experience and knowledge of recruitment and job applications, along with my ideas, are given in this book and, I hope, will prove useful to everyone. Young or old, skilled or unskilled, everyone needs sound strategies if they are to sell themselves successfully today.

In Britain the average advertised post now attracts 200 applicants, possibly more. Employers have plenty of people from whom to choose, so good applications, research, choosing the right type of post and putting yourself across in the best possible way are very important. Employers have little time for applicants who are casual in their approach, or who have not thought out their application properly. Advertising and recruitment procedures cost money and time, so employers are understandably careful when sifting through letters and CVs to work out the short list for interviews.

This book shows you how to use up-to-date strategies to get your name onto that interview shortlist, and then how to make good use of your interview. No-one can wave a magic wand, but with thought and application, following the ideas in this book, you should obtain the desired result!

'What Have I To Offer?'
Be aware of your strengths! Without confidence in your abilities and skills it is almost impossible to convince any prospective employer of your worth. If you cannot sell yourself to yourself, then you will not sell yourself to an employer. Being confident and positive are all-important in today's job market. That is not to say that arrogance is needed, nor blasé optimism, but inner confidence and self-esteem are your prime weapons in the contest.

Positive factors in the job hunter can be divided into

two basic types:

1. Specific job skills
2. General life skills

Both are important. Specific job or occupational skills can include qualifications, experience, specialist knowledge of an area of commerce, science or industry, a driving licence and knowledge of roads, language ability, possession of recognised professional certificates, etc.

General life skills are even more diverse, and sometimes may overlap the specific occupational skills: age, being physically fit, communication skills, the ability to get on with members of the public, dexterity, social background, appearance, hobbies, outside interests and so on. It is important to identify those areas which are your strongest factors and to use them, drawing attention to them at relevant points in your application. It will depend upon the type of work for which you are looking. This process of gearing your skills, experience and abilities to job applications is known as 'slanting', and I make much use of the idea of slanting in this book.

Age is one factor which tends to dwell in the minds of many. For some, the negative aspects of age often seem to outweigh the positive advantages and people rule themselves out before even beginning.

If you are an older job seeker, think about your age positively, like this:

Your attitude to change is good, you are flexible and able to learn new skills.
Your health is good.
You are eager to continue working for many years to come and you are keen to put your skills and experience to use.
You are settled and unlikely to move on.
You have mature judgment and common sense.

You have a proven work record, are punctual and
    reliable.
You are experienced in dealing with other people.

If you fall into the younger age group then make use of
your youth in the following way:

You are seeking a post on a long term basis.
You are keen to prove yourself and therefore you would
    be a good employee.
You are eager, enthusiastic and motivated.
Your physical abilities are at their best and will remain so
    for many years to come.
You are not restricted to previous employers' routines and
    procedures.
You are adaptable and quick to learn.

Although some employers do prefer younger applicants, there are advantages to employing an older person.
Many occupations demand a certain maturity and require
responsibility which is sometimes lacking in younger
people.

The important thing is to think positively about your
age. Always remember that there are two sides to any
question.

Job hunters often overlook the importance of transferable skills. These are skills common to all (or at least
several) occupational areas. Punctuality, work discipline,
the ability to work on your own initiative, make decisions
and deal with people from all backgrounds are just a few
examples. Transferable skills form an important part of
any job seeker's *skills profile*.

Take a little time to draw up a list of your transferable
skills for use in applications. Don't forget that skills
gained through hobbies or out-of-work interests can also
be useful when applying for employment: involvement in
social activities, tenants' association, sports clubs, handi-
crafts, etc. Such information adds depth to an application.

I give below a list of suggested transferable skills from
which you can select any which are relevant, and to which
you should add your own ideas.

Transferable Skills

communication skills
organisational ability
numeracy
physically fit
diplomatic
smart appearance
firm/authoritative
able to follow instructions
non-smoker
good knowledge of road
   routes
honest
flexible on hours
own transport
good socialiser
good public speaker

typing/keyboard skills
analytical skills
language abilities
full driving licence
friendly
mature approach
polite
able to learn and develop
respectful of premises
patient
able to work to timetables
attention to detail
good telephone manner
able to do simple repairs
able to work unsupervised

Leisure Skills

writing
painting
managing a sports team
conservation work
making clothes
DIY
youth work
community work
gardening
Neighbourhood Watch
making children's toys
amateur dramatics

photography
travel
running a club
car maintenance
metalwork
cooking
Special Constable
T.A.V.R.
painting and decorating
St. John's Ambulance
   Brigade

Achievements

represented city in sports   won medals for a hobby

saved a life
organised a charity event
gained a licence
won competitions
participated in charity events
taught yourself a new skill
learned to play a musical
   instrument
completed a correspondence
   course

published author
passed examinations
stopped a crime
completed a marathon
R.L.S.S. bronze medallion
advanced driving test
coached other people
long distance walking
Open University
raised sponsorship

How to make use of your transferable skills, whether they are drawn from work or leisure, is our next concern. What, for instance, could be the relevance of stamp collecting to any job other than working in a Philately shop?

Well, first you have to consider the skills involved in stamp collecting: organising materials, reading and researching, care of the collection, attention to detail, collecting information from a wide range of sources, homing in on the relevant areas. All these are skills which are needed in a variety of posts: administration, research, information collection and dissemination and record keeping.

Another example is playing soccer for a local Sunday league football team. The transferable skills here include being physically fit, following a set of rules and instructions, abiding by the decisions of the referee, attending training sessions on a regular basis, competing in a fair and friendly manner and socialising afterwards. Discipline, routine, motivation and punctuality – all these are part of playing football and they also happen to be essential work discipline skills.

Transferable skills may also exist where similar tasks are involved in different jobs. You may have been employed as a sales person in a shop, serving customers, handling cash and completing related paperwork. You could apply for a post as a delivery driver for a courier service, delivering parcels to customers' homes, handling damaged goods, related paperwork, returns and daily checks on the vehicle. Transferable skills would include the ability to deal with customers in a polite and tactful manner, smart appearance, accuracy and experience of documentation.

From these examples I hope you can begin to see the value of transferable skills, drawn from leisure interests and previous employment. Obviously, specific work skills play the greater part in performance of any given job, but employers will often take other factors, from an applicant's background and skills profile, into consideration. A candidate who is involved in community work on a voluntary basis, and who gives time to provide services and facilities for others, is obviously a motivated individual who could bring some of that motivation to bear in a job. If the community work involves administration, organising funding, advertising or staff control, then the applicant possesses extremely useful skills, relevant to a variety of jobs.

Everyone has something to offer. It is important to identify your strong points and to make full use of them. Look at any application form and you will see questions such as 'What do you feel you can offer this company?', or 'Give examples of your experience in handling members of the public', and 'Give reasons why you feel you should be considered for this post.'

Work skills and hobby experience can say something about people: their ability to learn, to adapt to new situations, determination, health, personality, dexterity, ability with measurements, with words, and personal motivation. All these are important elements in the make-up of the successful candidate.

To help you organise your information it is a good idea to list your work and non-work skills, detailing any equipment you can use, special tasks you have successfully undertaken in work or in leisure, achievements and awards or personal feelings of satisfaction gained, and why. These will provide a useful base for information in application forms, letters and interviews.

Long-Term Unemployed

People who have been out of work for a long period (6 months or more at the time of writing) are put into this category by the Government Employment Services. But it does not necessarily carry such a stigma as many people might at first think. Employers are happy to consider candidates who have been out of the employment market for some time provided that they can account for their absence and can show that they are ready to return to work.

Such people can benefit from special schemes, run by Employment Services, which can channel them into work. Many employers are now actively involved in schemes such as the Job Interview Guarantee scheme, Customised Employment Training, Work Trials and Employment Action, all designed to favour the long-term unemployed. Many people who have been out of work for some time may feel their situation presents barriers to employment, but they have much to offer any employer. With the right approach they can be just as effective in their applications as people who are changing jobs or have been out of work a few weeks. One thing about them is that they will be very eager to return to work, and often are more flexible than people who have only recently become unemployed. They are often more likely to stay in a post once they have been taken on, and will have completed training courses to learn new skills or upgrade their existing ones; something which newly-redundant people will not be able to offer.

If you have been out of work for some time it is important to make sure that you account for your unemployment honestly and openly. Draw attention to your efforts to get back into work, training, education, voluntary work etc. Make sure that you are prepared to discuss any long gaps in your work history with an employer.

Don't take the attitude that you would prefer not to talk about your periods out of work, or refuse to discuss them completely. This will only give employers the wrong impression, and leave them to make their own conclusions about you (which will probably be unfavourable).

Don't forget the importance of initiatives such as voluntary work and part-time study, but don't give the impression that you have spent the last five years or more simply studying part-time with no real objective.

If you can, apply for temporary work, because it often leads to permanent posts. Offer to complete a work trial with an employer. The JIG Team (Job Interview Guarantee Team) at local Employment Service offices will be able to arrange these.

If you find that employers do not reply, or reject you frequently, then attend a job search course such as a Job Club, or a Job Plan Workshop. This will help you to identify any faults you may have in your approach to employers and sharpen your application skills. Attendance at a Job Club will also help you to maintain a routine and will impress employers. The free facilities will enable you to make many more applications than you could afford to make on your own.

Coming Back To Work
Some people may have been out of work for reasons other than being made redundant and the poor job opportunities in their area. They may have been recently released from prison, and are starting to look for work, or they may have been physically or mentally ill, and have spent some time under treatment in a hospital. Also, many women spend years away from work to raise children to at least school age. They may feel that their absence from full time work stops them from picking up their former employment, and that their skills are inappropriate to the current work environment.

Anyone falling into the above groups *can* succeed in

their job search and get back into employment. As with people who have been long-term unemployed, special schemes are operated by Employment Services to help cater for the specific groups of job seekers.

Ex-Offenders

People who have been released from prisons, borstals and remand prisons, and even people who have convictions but have not served prison sentences, may experience specific problems.

Anyone who falls into this category should get specialist help. A useful organisation to contact is NACRO (National Association for the Care and Rehabilitation of Offenders). Consult your careers library and the telephone directory to find your local branch.

The main problem most offenders experience is that of *declaration*, or explaining offences to employers. Many people find it difficult to explain their crimes, and either try to deceive employers by not telling them, or try to make light of their offence and play it down. Neither strategy is particularly popular with employers. Nor might pleading innocence win favour.

The Rehabilitation of Offenders Act 1974 was designed to help people in this situation. It gives guidelines on when an applicant is required to tell an employer about convictions.

The full Act is too long to quote here, but basically most offences, receiving not more than 2½ years in prison, are 'spent' after a period of rehabilitation. The rehabilitation period for a prison sentence of 6 months up to 2½ years is 10 years; for a prison sentence less than 6 months it is 7 years; and for a fine or other sentence it is 5 years. These periods are halved if the person convicted was under 17 at the time. When an offence is 'spent', the applicant does not have any legal obligation to tell an employer, even if the employer asks about convictions. If the employer does find out at a later date, he cannot legally take action against the individual.

Certain occupations are exempt from the Rehabilitation Act: teaching, medical work, accounts, Law, care work (including voluntary posts) and the Gaming and Betting Industry. Application forms for these occupations will state that the post is exempt from the Rehabilitation Act, and will require details of convictions, dates and sentences. The Act covers offences which receive fines, probation orders, and custodial sentences. There are separate sections for young adults under 17 years of age. You can get advice about the Rehabilitation Act in libraries, careers services, from local Probation Services and Employment Services offices. Certain categories of offence are not covered by the Act, and some ex-offenders may need professional advice.

Long-Term Hospital Leavers

People who have spent a long time in hospital or mental hospital may also experience difficulties in job applications. Accounting for their absence from the labour market is not quite so difficult as for ex-offenders, but many ex-patients, particularly from mental institutions, feel embarrassed to discuss their illness.

The first point to remember is that everyone can fall ill, and the fact that you have undergone treatment is a point in your favour. If the illness has now been completely cleared up then you must make sure that you state this in your applications. If there is still some doubt about your potential as an employee, then it is important that you get some advice from your doctor or specialist concerning your limitations. It may be that your former work is no longer available to you on health grounds. In that case a new career, and possibly training first, are the necessary steps to take.

Some illnesses are recognised by Employment Services and the Department of Social Security, and anyone who is eligible may register as partly, or fully, disabled. People registered disabled often receive preferential treatment from some employers, notably public sector organisations.

Mental illness patients may also experience problems when applying for work. Some people are very conscious of the stigma which attaches in our society to mental illness and the use of psychiatrists.

In many countries psychiatrists are used as regularly as dentists (in America, for instance). The idea that anyone who has consulted a psychiatrist or spent some time in a mental hospital is necessarily unstable is completely unfounded. Employers are quite willing to consider applications from ex-mental patients in exactly the same way that they consider applications from people who have been physically ill – they need to be assured that the applicant is fit to undertake the duties required of them. If your hospital stay was ordered by a court then the Rehabilitation of Offenders Act will apply.

If the mental illness was job related, then a move to another kind of work may be necessary. If a person cracks because of pressure, re-employing them in the same situation may only lead to a recurrence of the same problems. Re-training may be a sensible option, linked to voluntary work to ease the transition from hospital to full time employment. Special courses may be provided in your area to rehabilitate long-term hospital patients and to teach vocational skills and assess potential alternative jobs. Employment Services would know about any such courses, and the hospital or Health Authority may provide the course or may have a contract with a local TEC (Training Enterprise Council) to provide this kind of help.

The main thing is to make sure that you can talk in an interview about your hospital stay without hesitation. Make your answer definite and to the point, stating postively that the treatment is finished now and that you are 100% fit again.

If you are undergoing out-patient treatment, state that this will not interfere with your work if you are taken on. Visit the Disablement Registration Officer in your local Job Centre and get some advice from your doctor. Visit a careers library and check out alternative employment and courses available to help you re-enter employment.

Women Returners
Women who have been away from the job market due to family commitments may feel that they have little to offer employers. This group is often known as Women Returners. They feel that their skills and experience are no longer valid in the employment market, simply because they have been at home for some years. This is completely inaccurate. Running a house and bringing up children require skills which are essential in the workplace: planning, organisation, timetables, self-discipline, enthusiasm and stamina.

Special courses and initiatives exist to help Women Returners overcome their problems, real or perceived. Local TECs will almost certainly offer courses catering for women, either teaching job search skills or vocational training, or a combination. Some cities have women-only Job Clubs, and other initiatives such as Job Search Seminars may help identify options for the Woman Returner.

Voluntary work may also bridge the gap to employment, giving an opportunity to put skills to use in practical situations. Many female members of my Job Clubs are women returners, and lots of them have taken part-time courses and done voluntary work to improve their skills and to get them back into a work-situation routine.

It is important to make sure that any dependent children are catered for when a mother returns to work. Contingency planning is important: what happens if a child falls ill and cannot attend school? Some larger organisations provide crêche facilities for children of pre-school age, and play leaders for the school holidays, to assist working mothers.

The amount of time a working mother can give to employment needs assessing before applications are made. It is worth talking to a claimant advisor about in-work benefits and Family Credit for anyone with children who wants to return to work.

For women returning to work after bringing up a family to young adulthood the situation is simpler, but the gap in employment may be much greater. Courses to assess your skills and offer guidance are useful. Many women have successfully trained in new occupations and found employment after sixteen or more years as a housewife.

Choosing The Job For You

This section may not be necessary for all readers; you may already be certain what kind of work you are looking for. In that case, go straight to Part 3 (page 40), and start considering your CV.

The kind of job you apply for will depend upon a combination of factors: skills, experience, locality, availability of the chosen work, general life skills, ambitions and expectations. You should want to obtain not just any old job, but an occupation which will give you satisfaction and reward. We spend most of our lives at work, so it is important to choose an occupation which will not only pay enough money, but also offer job satisfaction, perhaps the chance for promotion or development, and maintain interest and motivation. Select a suitable post or career path. Focus your attention and activities in a realistic and efficient manner; don't waste time and effort on unrealistic job choices.

Choosing a career or job change needs careful thought. There are many sources of information and advice available, including careers services and libraries, private consultants, publications and Government organisations.

Careers Libraries

One way to choose a new career or job is to visit a careers library and carefully analyse the information on hand there. Most cities and large towns have a careers library and careers service, usually free to any member of the public. They contain a wide range of information on jobs, training, skill requirements, etc. and useful addresses. The benefits of systematic reading in careers libraries cannot be over-emphasised; often the quick glance at a career booklet can result in further interest and an eventual successful application.

Many careers libraries offer advice from Careers Guidance Counsellors. These are people trained in Occupational Guidance, with a good knowledge of the labour market and many different careers, who can help you with your decision. Their advice is based on experience and careful training. Many careers services also use computer programs to aid analysis and processing of their clients' details.

Careers Computer Programs

These systems are used by a variety of agencies. One word of advice about using computer programs to identify job choice or training opportunities: computers do not 'think'. They simply work on the information fed into them in their programmed manner. Hence, whenever you allow your information to be used in a computer system, always keep this reservation in mind.

Questionnaires for computer career programs can be quite broad, and different answers can be read to give different conclusions. Most career services use their computer systems as a supplement to their advisors, but beware of any totally computer-devised career choice. Use computer career information as a suggestion for further research and investigation, involving career booklets, counselling and personal contact with people working in that particular occupation.

Private Career Consultants

These vary in price and services offered. Fees may be from around £50 to several hundred for the prestigious companies. Their main custom comes from executive and managerial clients, although their client group may have widened somewhat with changes in the employment situation.

If you wish to use a private consultant, shop around. Try to get an exact idea of the services on offer: some companies charge large amounts of money for a service which is little better than you could provide for yourself using public facilities.

At the other end of the spectrum there are very professional consultants who use complex tests to identify client skills, and then provide advice, action-planning, a CV and copies. Generally prices are higher in London, but prestigious consultancies may charge highly elsewhere.

Before you commit any money, find something out about the people running the consultancy: are they experienced recruitment/careers advisors? What are their qualifications? Generally a careers advisor should possess the Diploma in Careers Guidance, which is the recognised careers advisory certificate, or perhaps membership of the Institute of Careers Advisors or the Institute of Personnel Management. Ideally they should also have good commercial/industrial experience upon which to draw, and they may include Psychometric testing as part of their service.

There are also several career choice publications on offer, and these can usually be found in libraries and careers service buildings. They offer insights into new options and career paths for anyone not sure about their best direction.

Academic Libraries
Library facilities at Universities and local Further Education Colleges are usually open to members of the public. They will hold information on large companies as well as useful technical and professional publications. College and University careers services may also be open to the public, although actual counselling is probably restricted to students and graduates of the institution. If you are

looking for management level work within a specific profession or area of commerce, college facilities may stock relevant professional publications and journals which are difficult to buy from newsagents.

Remember that campuses are often split into different locations, and the library will contain books and journals which reflect the dominant courses at any particular campus site. You may have to travel to another part of town or another campus to see a particular publication.

Spare Time Interests

Spare time interests can be useful in your job search for their transferable skills. But the hobby, or something closely related, may exist as a job in its own right, and a keen amateur could perhaps adopt a more professional standing.

Examples would be the keen DIY enthusiast who takes a job selling decorating and building equipment in a shop, or someone who is keen on electronics and hi-fi construction working in an audio repair shop. Identify a close job choice and check to see if you need training to develop your skills before you can apply.

Develop Yourself And Improve Your Prospects

Self-development may involve learning new skills or brushing up existing ones. You might participate in activities which contribute to job hunting: gaining experience through voluntary work, keeping fit and alert, practising presentation skills, etc.

By developing your skills you will have more to offer an employer, and you prevent yourself getting 'rusty'. You will also develop a set of activities which will keep you busy and make it easier for you to return to the work routine.

Ideas for self-development include:

Part-Time Study

Full-Time Study
Voluntary Work
Sports and Leisure
Practising Writing and Speaking

Even if the activities you choose are not particularly job related, they will benefit your applications. If you are unemployed they are particularly useful. Employers will see that you have a routine, you will meet people, possibly make useful contacts and you will have something to say about yourself.

Part-Time Study
If you feel that your occupational skills are not up to scratch then there are many courses on offer to improve vocational abilities, teach new technology and equipment and to prepare you for today's job market. Courses are run by: local authority colleges, the Workers' Educational Association, community workshops and Universities. Some develop specific occupational skills, others are more general. It should be possible, subject to provision in your area, to learn useful skills by part-time study, and provide a good base from which to develop occupational choice.

Prices vary: local authority colleges and WEA courses are the cheapest, private business colleges and correspondence courses the most expensive. Some private colleges offer discounts for anyone unemployed, and local authority colleges usually make special arrangements for people on a low income or claiming unemployment benefit. Course duration also varies. Local authority colleges run longer courses, over a year or more, while private training companies and business colleges offer short, intensive courses, designed to achieve levels of competence more quickly. Private colleges, and some local authority colleges, run flexible, modular courses, offering a variety of attendance times. An example would be morning-only courses to cater for mothers with children to pick up from school.

All can expand their skills. Identify relevant courses and decide where to study. Consider cost, availability and time. Course providers publish details in a prospectus, available from the institutes themselves, and often also from libraries. Some courses run on a workshop system, with term enrolments, rather than the traditional annual enrolment.

You may decide to use the National Vocational Qualification framework to gain a recognised qualification, or to claim accreditation for activities in a previous job. Under this you are assessed by qualified adjudicators, who observe your performance in paid or voluntary roles and award the appropriate level in the NVQ awards. Many employers recognise the validity of the NVQ certificates which are based on performance related achievements, rather than academic or vocational training in a college. The NVQ levels start at 1 and go up to 5, with level 5 being judged equivalent to degree level.

Some volunteer organisations may fund NVQ assessments for their volunteers, and Training for Work placements and Careerships placements can involve NVQ accreditation. Young people can claim NVQ assessments for free. Details of NVQ providers can be found with TECs, Careers Information Services and colleges.

Full-Time Study

This can be with Further Education Colleges, Universities or private institutions. Financial support is important: local authority grants for young students are now topped up by Student Loans, and re-payment of the loan must be allowed for.

Many institutions encourage mature students (anyone over 23 years old) and special arrangements may be made for anyone lacking formal entry requirements. These may include Access Courses, which lead the mature student through a preparatory course, often tailored to the main subject. Alternatively, a short test or production of a piece of academic work may be accepted in lieu of A-levels or equivalents. Entry to full-time study for the mature applicant will also depend on past activity: part-time study, employment, voluntary work etc. will influence the selectors.

The subject and aim of a course are also important. There are courses which train people for specific vocational careers, such as legal executives, or laboratory technicians or medical secretaries. Other courses may be more general with broader objectives and no specific vocational target: English Literature, History, or some Art and Design courses. These courses develop academic ability and knowledge, and useful transferable skills, but do not open up a definite career path. Further study, with a specific occupational objective, is still required.

Full-time study must be entered with these points in mind. Of course, after three years at University the employment situation may be different. But it may not, and three years' study is a lot of time and energy to spend just to be back where you began. Unemployed graduates may be tempted to take a higher degree and return to the employment market later, better qualified. But University careers officers' surveys show that most employers are not interested in Post Graduate Qualifications unless they are the very best. Most prefer a graduate with a BA or BSc.

Voluntary Work
Not only is this enjoyable and rewarding but it is beneficial in many ways: it enables you to try out a new type of job, keep skills in practice, add to your experience or simply to get out of the house. Voluntary work can also get you a reference, which people who have been out of work for some time can find difficult to obtain.

There may even be an application form to fill in and perhaps a short informal interview, which are good practice for paid positions.

Voluntary work may be arranged by local volunteer bureaux, or by charitable agencies, community centres, churches or Tenants' Associations. There are also some Government agencies involved, such as Employment

Action. Organisations involved in the care of certain groups of disadvantaged people in our society also organise volunteer activity: the National Deaf Association, the Royal National Institute for the Blind, and Riding for the Disabled are good examples. Some of these organisations require specific skills and experience from their voluntary workers, others will run training courses to equip helpers. Some may require no more than reliability and a sympathetic ear.

Unemployed people, in particular, can gain from voluntary work, as they may add to their references. Also, volunteer work can break the routine of unemployment. It should not interfere with receipt of benefits such as Income Support or Unemployment Benefit, so long as your voluntary work does not take up too much time and interfere with your job search. If you are on state benefit contact your Claimant Advisor at the benefit office, before taking up voluntary work, and check the rules about how many hours per week you may do while remaining eligible for benefit.

Recruitment in certain occupations is often done directly from the volunteer workforce. This is especially the case in activities where volunteer input is relied upon heavily, such as drug or alcohol abuse counselling, probation work with ex-offenders and social work.

Volunteer work can be varied and stimulating: decorating, building, conservation work, working with the elderly, driving a mini-bus, coaching or training people, running a crèche or organising activities for children. Just a few hours of your time given to voluntary work can have a very positive effect on your job search, increasing your own self-esteem and widening your work experience.

Practising Presentation Skills
Practise your handwriting before making any applications. A few hours' work will soon improve your standards. Also practise printing in block capitals for completing application forms. Needless to say, good presentation in written applications is vital. In your previous job your colleagues may have learned to recognise your handwriting and read it

easily, but to a new employer it may present difficulties. Good standards will increase your chance of a favourable response.

Practising your speech can also improve your presentation skills. Think about how you speak. Identify any speech problems by recording yourself and then playing the cassette back. Mock interviews, with a friend, or simply reading out sample answers to standard questions will help with your oral skills; get used to speaking about typical interview topics. There are numerous relevant books available from libraries on communication skills, both verbal and non-ver bal (body language).

Keeping Fit And Alert
A little light exercise on a regular basis will benefit your appearance and performance at interviews. Exercise will keep your mind alert and enable you to deal with applications and interviews more efficiently. It is not necessary to try for a four-minute mile! Gentle strolling, swimming or light weight-training will result in a better frame of mind and a more alert and positive outlook. This will be transmitted at the interview. Anyway, for anyone who is unemployed a break from the boredom is necessary, and there are many sports which can be done cheaply. Local Authority sports halls often have special discount arrangements for people who are out of work.

Conclusion
I have taught these concepts to many unemployed people who have found them useful and productive. I have helped individuals, unemployed for 10 years, who have sat so long in their house they forgot what it was like to have a routine and deal with other people. These ideas remotivated them to pick up their search for employment.

In short, these ideas have worked for people I know personally and they can work for you!

PART TWO

MOTIVATION AND PLANNING FOR CHANGE

Why Change Jobs?

People change jobs for a variety of reasons: to improve their promotion prospects or pay; because of a change in health or personal circumstances; or even a relocation of the family home. Some people change jobs on a regular basis simply because they like variety, and are prepared to forfeit the benefits of long-term security for the challenge of new environments, possibly involving travel.

For the majority of people, changing jobs requires careful consideration. It is a good exercise to sit down and ask yourself *why* you wish to change your job. What would you expect to gain from a change? What might you lose?

There is no point changing posts just to find that the same problems recur. It is important to identify exactly why you feel the need to move on; then analyse these reasons. Are you simply running away from a situation that will follow you?

Almost everyone experiences periods of frustration and boredom with their job (the "Monday morning blues"). It is important that you do not make a hasty decision based on a short-term problem which may diminish in importance the next day.

'Am I Blocked?'

For many people, changing jobs is a necessary step in career advancement. Despite claims to the contrary, upward social mobility and career development are seldom achieved through service with a single employer. For the ambitious, movement from one job to another is often the key to success.

Deciding when it is a good time to move jobs requires some analysis. The state of your particular industry is obviously the important factor: recruitment levels, profits, amount of activity and the general outlook in your sector are good indicators of the situation, and of any likely opportunities available. Also take stock of the current progress of your career. What have you to offer another employer in a similar field? What do you expect to get in return for moving jobs and bringing your particular skills to another employer?

Before deciding that your only chance of advancement is to move jobs, consider fully all the prospects and opportunities available with your present employer. Many companies have strict policies of promotion from within, possibly in-house training to equip employees with skills for higher, more responsible posts. If your employer offers these kinds of opportunities then you may find that your career is best served by making use of them. Changing jobs can have disadvantages, and an unnecessary move may actually be a setback. For example, smaller firms may not afford the chances for promotion and career development which a larger company can provide.

If your current post offers no opportunities for advancement, if you have already exhausted the options open, or if you feel that you are being constantly passed over for promotion, then movement outward, to another organisation is required.

You will need to do thorough research into which companies and organisations offer something better than your present situation.

You may reply to advertisements or apply on a

speculative basis. Support your application carefully with reasons for your move. If you are too critical of your present post and employer then you may give a negative impression. Statements like: 'I applied for the higher management course but they put in Peter Jones instead, and he's only been with the company for a year! I'm always being passed over!' will cause suspicion in the minds of new employers. Why are you being passed over? Is there a problem which you have not mentioned?

Be positive about your desire to move. If you feel that you have expanded as much as your present post will allow, then mention this, but don't be too critical about your post. Say something good about your experiences with your present employer; state how you feel you have developed in your post, and where you feel a new post and employer could take you. If it is possible, stress that movement between employers is a rare event for you, only undertaken when absolutely necessary. The majority of employers regard frequent mobility as a danger sign; stability and loyalty in the workforce are valued criteria and should not be ignored. The company you apply to should feel that they are special, and that you are genuinely interested in them and are prepared to stay for some time.

There are some exceptions to these ideas: in certain industries people move from firm to firm and back again. Often in these instances the individual is expected to bring something to his or her new employer – usually clients. Hence there can be frequent movement between posts. Certain types of sales posts are notable for this system of recruitment and customer acquisition.

Pitfalls In Changing Jobs
Some of the problems with changing posts have already been touched on. One of the main points to consider is whether your move is absolutely necessary. Are you just trying to run away from a situation or problem which

should be dealt with now, thus making your present post better?

This was the case with a young sales manager I met a couple of years ago. He was totally depressed with his work, his achievement levels were low, and he generally felt bad about his job. Only a few years before he had enjoyed his work and had a much better achievement level. Why had his outlook changed so much? The reason was the new staff who had joined the firm. Some of them were his juniors, but because he was generous and amiable they had begun to take advantage of him. The result was that he was doing work which his staff should have done, over-stressing himself and losing control of the situation. He had come to believe that the only solution was to move to another job, or another kind of work completely.

He asked me about moving jobs. After talking to him I realised that his best interest would be served by regaining control in his present post and ironing out the problems with his staff. I told him to talk to his seniors and request their support. He would then at least have tried to use the options available to him instead of simply running away to avoid confrontation. Only if this failed would moving to another post be an acceptable alternative.

It is important that you do not change jobs on trivial grounds. In every post there are duties which are tedious or unpleasant, colleagues who may be awkward to deal with, clients who are rude or impatient. You should address problems like these directly or you may be changing jobs because you feel unhappy in your post for the rest of your working career.

Another major problem is too frequent movement. Every time a new member of staff or management joins a company or organisation there is a period of 'settling in', as the existing workforce and the newcomer get to know each other. If an employer has a constant procession of people joining the workforce it is difficult to achieve a cohesive unit. Production and industrial relations suffer.

Most employers prefer to employ people with a fairly good record of stable employment, although there are exceptions. In times of high unemployment these standards are sometimes relaxed, as many people take temporary posts to 'fill in', or accept posts which may not be entirely satisfactory, but generally, excessive movement between employers is not a good thing.

Anyone who shows evidence of over-frequent movement can be regarded as unstable and unsuitable for long-term development. It is difficult to state any valid time span, but changing jobs more than twice in two years is probably too much. A good work history should include posts held for at least two or three years, unless they were of a temporary nature or were taken with short term objectives in mind. For example, a recent graduate might take a job as a chamber maid or a bar person, with the intention of earning a little money until a better and more appropriate post becomes available. That sort of movement is acceptable, but some people never seem to settle down, and that deters employers.

An applicant whose CV shows numerous job changes may be unsettled, and liable to move on regularly. They may also have problems which no employer would relish the idea of inheriting. In some industries, such as banking and security work, frequent job changers are actually a security risk, and applications are only considered from people with reasonably stable backgrounds.

Employers imagine all kinds of things about people who frequently change jobs: about problems in their previous posts, or in their relationships with their employers or colleagues. Perhaps the short-term jobs mentioned are fictitious, or the applicant untrustworthy. These are all serious considerations for an employer and many of them will go straight on to the next applicant.

Every time you move, you will have to adapt to a new working environment, new relations, a new route to work, new pay arrangements, etc. Of course, all this can be rewarding and challenging, and is often part of the incentive for change. On the other hand, a new job can bring new stresses; you have to deal with new workmates, handle new routines and procedures, make sure that you pass your trial period and get on with your new employer.

For this reason, frequent job changes can lead to poor references, as short-term employers may not feel able to give an accurate assessment of your worth. As a Job Club leader I have frequently seen how, despite having a long work history, applicants are left high and dry without a substantial reference to support them.

Domestic routines may also have to be changed to accommodate the requirements of your new post, travel costs may alter, parking may not be easily available. As a newcomer you may be treated differently from the established workforce, and it may take some time before you are fully one of the team. These are points to consider carefully. (See also **Starting Your New Post** in Part 6, on page 120.)

Keeping It Secret
It is often important that you do not let your desire for change become common knowledge. Employers like loyalty, and an employee who breaks ranks and makes efforts to move can become devalued. If you go for a couple of posts and then find that your best interests are served by staying where you are, you do not want your standing to be reduced by it being known that you applied for other jobs.

There are also other reasons for secrecy. For instance, in times of high unemployment people are often very eager to get friends or relatives into jobs. News on the grapevine that you are looking for another post can cause a flurry of applications for your own job and your situation can be compromised. Even if you subsequently decide to stay with your company, chances for advancement, or even your current treatment, can be clouded by your application to other employers, particularly if they are competitors.

Then there is the 'domino effect'. The fact that an employee is looking for another job can be unsettling on colleagues, encouraging them to do the same. Many employers therefore prefer that if you must look for another job, you should at least be discreet, and not unnecessarily influence others to do the same.

Another danger is that other people in your organisation might also, secretly, be wanting to move. If you let them know that there is a possible opening available with another employer, they might apply themselves and take the job away from you.

Strategies for keeping your intentions secret are important. Obviously interviews have to be held at a time convenient to the prospective employer. The majority of job interviews are held in normal office hours, although there may be exceptions. If this conflicts with your present working arrangements, then some excuse must be made to account for your absence. Booking a day's leave is an obvious one, but doing this on a regular basis can arouse suspicion. It is best to try to cover your tracks by letting slip some story about visiting relatives, or a decorating job which will help to explain your days off. Another alternative, though one which has to be used carefully, is taking a day off and phoning in to say that you are ill. This should only be done as a last resort. It is against the rules of all employers. There is the danger that someone might see you travelling to or from your interview, and gossip can soon spread. You also leave yourself open to reports by anyone who bears you a grudge, or who fancies your job for themselves.

If an application form asks you if your present employer may be contacted as a reference before or after an interview, always say afterwards. That way, if you are not successful at the interview, or if you decide not to progress your application for some reason, your employer will not have been contacted unnecessarily.

Try not to read job-related publications in working

hours. Nothing advertises your desire to get another job more clearly than poring over the vacancies in the newspaper in your lunch break. Avoid using your employer's facilities to make applications. Don't use WPs at work and don't photocopy your CV at work; apart from it being dishonest, you may leave pointers to other people about your activities and plans. Awkward though it might be, try to deter prospective employers from contacting you at work. Always imply that they should contact you at home or in writing. Many a secret job hunt has been exposed because of inquisitive switchboard operators!

Planned Movement
Movement between employers always looks more positive if it seems to have a plan behind it. Random, off-the-cuff decisions look poor and, again, suggest instability. Planned moves, often taking place over several years, suggest logical thinking by the applicant, with a definite objective at the end. This will impress an employer.

Hence, when you account for any movement between posts, make your movement look organised and effective, rather than *ad hoc*. Think of the reasons for your movement. Time spent doing this will benefit your applications. Make positive statements about any job changes, and conclude that the present move is the culmination of your objectives; make the employer feel assured that your movement is likely to stop with them.

Hang On To Your Entitlements
When you move make arrangements to protect any fringe benefits which accrued from your previous post(s). Pension entitlements should be transferable from one post to another, but it is important that you get professional advice concerning your pension, super-annuation or any other entitlements.

If you are not sure where to go for this kind of advice,

then contact either your local CAB (Citizens' Advice Bureau) or the local branch of FIMBRA, the overseeing body of financial advisors. If you are changing jobs due to redundancy, you will need advice on your entitlement to state benefits: Government Employment Offices can advise you on your situation, but independent advice might be useful.

You may also wish to advise your bank, building society and any finance companies of the change in your situation, so that you can make some arrangements about any payments you must still make whilst on a reduced income. If you approach lenders before you incur arrears then amicable relations can be maintained. If your loan or mortgage is linked to an insurance policy against redundancy, and you become unemployed, check the actions required of you to cover payments and tell the insurers what has happened.

If you are in the market for a new or first pension scheme, shop around and compare different companies' policies. Prefer pension schemes which can be moved from job to job with little fuss.

Work Out The Perks

In many jobs some sort of extra payment, on top of the salary, is common. These fringe benefits or 'perks' often add up to a considerable sum, even in jobs at low levels: free parking, subsidised meals, business expenses, training allowances, flexi-time, amount of annual leave, overtime, bonuses, free/subsidised clothing, staff discounts, concessionary car insurance, cheap mortgage facilities, non-contributory pensions, health insurance, membership of professional bodies, concessionary social/sports club membership, etc.

The wise job mover would therefore consider *all* the fringe benefits when assessing if a move is worthwhile. A new job may bring some new benefits, but you could lose others you currently enjoy. For example, the loss of travel or parking facilities can result in a sizeable hole in a new salary cheque. Also, changing location can affect your income. There will be the expense of moving house, possibly buying and selling property. The effects on you and your family must also be taken into account.

The cost of living varies from city to city, and a job which offers a higher salary, but is located in a more expensive part of the country, may turn out to be the same in real terms, or even worse, than your present post. London is an obvious example, where salaries could be nominally up to 50% higher than in the provinces. But the cost of living, travel to work, rents and property prices are so much more expensive, and job movers must take these factors into account.

On the other hand a move from one city to another can provide cheaper living costs and the chance to buy your 'dream home' (or at least a larger house) or enjoy facilities which may not be available in your current location. Many large organisations have moved out of expensive areas and re-located their headquarters in provincial towns partly for these reasons.

You can always discuss fringe benefits with a prospective employer, and if you have a lot to offer you might get a better package than currently. Generally employers will help with relocation costs where necessary. Travel concessions are common for long-distance commuters. Some posts allow a sort of 'settling in' payment, to help bridge the gap when changing jobs.

PART THREE

A RED-HOT CV FOR HIGH IMPACT

The Curriculum Vitae ('course of life') is a list of your employment details, education, achievements, personal details and leisure interests.

Advantages Of The CV

A well designed CV is a definite asset to anyone looking for work. Using one has many advantages:

It conveys information quickly.

Letters can be shorter (an advantage to both employer and job seeker).

Good quality photocopies are acceptable.

It can be a 'prompt list' for application forms, on the telephone and before interviews.

It can be included with speculative letters.

It gives employers a document to file for future reference.

There are no fixed rules about the production of a CV. It can vary in length; layout, content and order of information can be re-arranged to suit the individual's taste. The important thing is that the CV achieves its goal: to provide sufficient information on the applicant to interest the employer.

Basically there are two types of CV: the Chronological

CV, which orders information around dates, usually in reverse order. The second, less common, is the Achievement CV, which draws attention to your achievements and puts less emphasis on dates.

The chronological CV has the advantage that it presents information in a familiar way, while the achievement CV can work well if an applicant has moved jobs frequently, or has had little work experience.

The achievement CV emphasises the applicant's progression and success, in or out of work. Frequent job changes can be kept backstage, so to speak, and the best you have to offer is there to be read. A disadvantage with this kind of CV is that it is not the normal style. Employers might be left unsure about your work history if there are no dates to account for your activities but in some occupations this might not matter quite as much.

CVs in Britain were once the sole preserve of the executive or managerial job hunter, but they are now widely used. Advertisements usually require the applicant to include a CV with a covering letter.

Production Of A Well-Designed CV
A CV may be designed and produced by one of the many commercial agencies which offer this service, or you may design your own. Either way you must make sure that the CV is well presented and attractive and makes use of your information in the optimum way.

Commercially produced CVs vary in cost, style and presentation. Shop around and compare prices and quality. Some CV 'experts' are simply typing CVs with little attention to content or layout whilst charging hefty sums. Competition between CV agencies is fierce, and many companies claim that their particular CV design is unique and achieves results.

Some companies work on a 24 hour service, others take a little longer. They will give you details of their CV layout, prices and service, which will include an information sheet for you to fill in and return, post paid. The information you supply is then assembled, the most relevant sections selected and a CV constructed and returned to you for your approval. Some companies also re-vitalise existing CVs.

If you make your own CV it is a definite advantage to type it on a word-processor. This will allow you to hold it on disc and print a new version when required, without re-typing the whole document. If you can't afford a word-processor, borrow a friend's and keep a copy disc. Some libraries and colleges have WPs for public use at a nominal cost.

Quality of print and paper is important. Compare some quotes again. Ideally, any copies made for you by a CV agency (and the number will vary from one agency to another) should be on quality A4 size paper, 100 gsm, white laid or white wove cartridge. Some people prefer coloured paper, although this can produce poor quality photocopies. Art work around a CV may be useful, if it is relevant to the post.

CV agencies use various printers: daisy wheel, dot matrix, bubble-jet and laser print. Laser print is the best, producing sharp, well-defined copies, which also photocopy very well. Never accept a CV on perforated tractor-feed paper. Insist on quality cartridge paper.

Photocopies should be legible and clear of marks. Photocopiers in public places, such as libraries, are often heavily used and can give poor results. A printing or photocopying company will produce better quality copies but may cost more.

If you decide to use a CV company make sure that they really are designing a tailor-made document for you. A standard CV will not achieve the same result as one which has been carefully designed. Consider the length: a CV containing every bit of information would be too long for most people, so some selectivity is necessary. As a general rule, it should be from 1 side to 3 sides of A4 paper, depending on the style and layout chosen.

You should slant the information contained in your CV in order to direct the reader's attention and keep the length down to a sensible size. Careful consideration of its contents will result in a neat document which will get results. Have more than one version of your CV if you are applying for different types of post. Each version will emphasise the most relevant skills and abilities you have to offer for that particular calling. For example, one CV might stress your administration skills, keyboard facilities etc; another might draw attention to your communication skills and customer care experience.

I had two versions of my CV when I was looking for work, one slanted more to office and shop work, in which I paid attention to communication skills, job experience, personality and organisational abilities; the other version was geared more to training or lecturing posts, stressing my degree and my experience in delivering seminars.

You may choose to have a long and a short version of your CV, although I think a full CV is best for all your applications. One page CVs are either very cramped, making them difficult to read, or they are skimpy and fail to include enough information. My experience in running Job Clubs has taught me that the optimum size for a CV is about two sides of A4 paper, designed so that your information is arranged in logical sections.

So production of the CV is important. You need to consider carefully how best to do it to get job interviews. Below are some ideas about CVs which you can use when considering commercial examples, or designing your own.

PERSONAL DETAILS – name and address, date of birth, marital status, nationality (optional), health, National Insurance number.

EDUCATION – from age 12 or 13 upwards. Include name and address of school, dates attended and any qualifications gained. Further or Higher Education may be listed separately in the same manner.

TRAINING – not always applicable, but mainly the same kind of details as for education. Training courses completed with an employer (First Aid, Health and Safety At Work, Fire Fighting, or any Government Training Schemes such as ET or JTS or YT) could also be included.

EMPLOYMENT HISTORY – listing present and previous employment, voluntary work, temporary work, part-time work. Any placements gained from ET could also be listed in this section. Necessary details include dates of employment, name and address of employer, job title and brief details of your duties.

You don't necessarily need to list all your previous posts. It depends upon the amount of information you have to offer. Some people list those of the last five to ten years, other, younger candidates might not have five years' employment so their information will take up less space. A series of temporary posts could be abbreviated to save room.

For a chronological CV, begin with the most recent post or activity and go back through previous posts (although, on occasions, the opposite way, from school or college and first job can prove useful). Think what useful skills and abilities you used in previous work, what you achieved from these posts and how these ideas might interest prospective employers.

ADDITIONAL INFORMATION – a general heading which can include any relevant information not yet covered: car ownership, clean driving licence, language abilities. You might use this section to make a statement about yourself, your strengths and what you feel you can bring to the type of post for which you have applied.

LEISURE INTERESTS – sports, hobbies, membership of any clubs or teams, any awards gained, or personal satisfaction obtained. You might say what you feel you gain from any of your hobbies or sports that are relevant to the job.

REFERENCES – not always included but I think it is useful to put them in (with the referee's permission), as it could speed up the selection process. You need the referee's name and address, their relationship to you and their occupation. It is sensible to state if the referees can be contacted immediately or if they should be contacted after an interview.

Referees should have known you a reasonable amount of time: an ex-employer is best, although personal acquaintances, business people or ex-lecturers or trainers can also be valid referees.

Other sections which may be used in a CV include a PROFILE – a short statement about yourself and your experience and skills, usually about 6 lines long and inserted after personal details. Another optional section is ACHIEVEMENTS – any particular examples of promotion or good work performance, increases in efficiency or profitability for which you were responsible, either as an individual or as a member of a team.

Some of these areas overlap, and not every CV will require all of them. They are suggestions about the type of information you can include, depending on personal choice.

Give Consideration To The Layout

A CV is a 'list', but attention to the layout and appearance of the text is important. Too much information in a small space results in a solid block of type. Information should be split up and attractive to read. The optimum design is one which gives relevant information in a well-presented manner.

On the following pages are a few example CVs, ranging from a single side of A4 paper to longer designs which might run to 2 or 3. There are also some examples of CVs for particular individuals: someone with no specific experience or qualifications (page 52); a newly qualified graduate with no work experience (pages 53–54); a mother returning to the labour market after several years spent raising a family (pages 55–56); a person seeking manual work (page 57); a member of HM Forces returning to civilian life (pages 58–59); and an achievement CV for someone with a varied work history (page 60). Use these examples to help you design your own CV, or copy one of the designs completely.

Whatever design you use for your CV, make sure that it does the trick! A CV that covers every minute of your life is unlikely to appeal. Select relevant information. Present it in an attractive manner. Think of the personnel officer who has to read two hundred CVs every time the company advertises. If you were in their shoes how would you feel if you received a CV that was 10 pages long? Make things easy for the reader and you will win!

Example CVs That Hit The Mark

CURRICULUM VITAE

Susan Jane Thompson   43 Runcorn Avenue, Manchester
                           M8 5TY Tel: (0161) 531098

Age: 34   **Marital Status:** single
Nationality: British **Health:** excellent

Education
University of Manchester (year)–(year): B.Sc. Chemistry
grade: II:i. Dissertation: 'The Behaviour of Acids'
University of Manchester (year)–(year): M.Sc. Chemistry
and Applied Science. Thesis: Pharmaceutical Industry –
its objectives and issues.

Employment History
(year)–(year) Analytical Chemist: Trent Scientific
Services, The Institute Buildings, Wales Road,
Manchester M4 6EW
(year)–(year) Senior Laboratory Chemist: Lockwood
Chemical Corporation, 458 Victoria Avenue, Manchester
M2 6ON

Interests
Swimming, diving, literature, represented Manchester
University at the British University swimming
championships.

References
Dr T Yeomans, Chemistry Department, University of
Manchester.
Mrs G Rowland, Personnel Officer, Lockwood Chemical
Corporation.

CURRICULUM VITAE

Andrew David Watson   68 Bridge Street, Norwich,
Age: 45   N4 7PW Tel: (01603) 871390
Marital Status: married **Health:** excellent

Profile
Versatile administration manager with twenty years'
experience in the travel industry. Member of ABTA,
fluent in German and Italian, experienced in all aspects of
the travel and tourism business, computer literate, full
driving licence, able to re-locate.

Training
(year) – Training in Tourism certificate, levels 1 and 2.
Achieved distinction.
(year) – RSA 1, 2 and 3 in keyboarding and word
processing.
(year) – 'Computers in Tourism': a short course for travel
agents in computer booking systems.

Employment History
(year)–(year) Thomas Peckham Ltd. General Counter
Assistant, making bookings, related paperwork, display
of brochures.

(year)–(year) George Woodholme Travel Ltd. Trainee
Assistant Manager, promoted to senior assistant manager.
Running a busy travel agency, liaising with continental
travel agents and hotels.

(year)–date Susan Hampshire World Wide Travel
Agency. Manager for five branches of a busy travel
agency, specialising in travel to exotic locations.

Overseeing the branch managers' work, publicity and advertising and recruitment.

Leisure Interests
Driving, travel, languages and sport. Play squash regularly for a local club. I have visited the USA, Mexico, Sweden, Hong Kong, Australia and Japan.

References
Mr D Longden, Club Secretary, Firestone Sports and Social Club, 56 Tavistock Road, Norwich N5 9TP

Mr J F Senior, Area Manager, Susan Hampshire World Wide Travel Agency, 23 Victor Promenade, Norwich N7 4GH

Mrs H T Fisher, Personnel Manager, George Woodholme Travel Ltd, 12 Trent Road, Norwich N1 6DX

CURRICULUM VITAE

David George Holmes
456 The Meadows
Manchester
M12 4TP
(0161) 451830

Profile

Experienced sales manager with fifteen years' background in FMCG sales. Strong field sales techniques, good communicator, able to work to deadlines, motivate staff and train and recruit. Clean driving licence and good motorway experience. Member of the Institute of Marketing, hold HND Business Studies. 3 years in succession held the company award for the most successful sales manager. Guest speaker at the Tobacco Retailers' Annual Conference (year).

Employment History

January (year)–date: Sales Manager, Northern Territory, Green and Withenshawe, 56 The Green, Roland, Manchester M9 8RW
Duties: overseeing the field sales representative team, consisting of 34 salespeople, ensuring sales targets are met, training and recruiting, arranging opening discounts for new accounts, reporting to the directors on performance and targets.

March (year)–January (year): Assistant Sales Manager, Fowler and Thompson, 78–82 West Morland Avenue, Cheswick, Manchester M5 8VH
Duties: overseeing the field sales force, accompanying the sales manager on field trips, attending meetings, accounts work, training new staff, cold calling to generate new business, attending trade fairs and conventions.

Education
(year)–(year): Hurlingham Business College, Retford in Ashfield, Manchester M1 4RY
Qualification: HND Business Studies. Distinction.
Successful placement with George Rivelin & Co Ltd.

Personal Details

Age: 40   **Health:** excellent
Marital status: married   **Nationality:** British

Leisure Interests
Golf, driving, member of the East Hampton Country Club.

References

James Klein   Stephen Black
Personnel Officer   Councillor
Green and Withenshawe   23 Rose Avenue
56 The Green   Mirrfield
Roland   Manchester
Manchester   M17 5EB
M9 8RW

CURRICULUM VITAE

Daniel Stephen Clarke
26 Gainsborough Close
Retford
R13 5TT
Tel: (01777) 665213

Age: 16
School attended: St James' Comprehensive, 343 Gleadless
Common, Retford.
Dates: (year–year)
Achieved a good all-round education in English and
Mathematics, Woodwork and Physical Education.
Attendance and punctuality excellent. Achieved merit
award for politeness and good attitude.
Out of school activities: Member of school Football
Team, represented school in county league competition.
Library helper for one year.

Interests: Football, cycling, youth club activities.
Maintaining my bicycle.

Future plans: Enrolled for evening classes to improve
woodwork skills and have applied to Blackheath Junior
Amateur Football Team for a trial.

General skills: Physically fit, sensible attitude, can follow
instructions and perform any task willingly. Good
handwriting and basic numeracy, polite and of smart
appearance. Enjoy practical jobs.

Reference: Mr D Jacobs, Head Teacher, St James'
Comprehensive.

CURRICULUM VITAE

Simon J Thompson
Age: 22
Nationality: British

29 Victor Avenue
Crawford
Suffolk
C6 7TR
(01733) 772331

Education
(year)–(year) The University of North Yorkshire, Leeds,
L1 4WW

Qualifications: BA(Hons) History and Economics,
achieved II:ii.

Course details: The BA(Hons) History and Economics
course consisted of written work, seminar presentation, a
written project of 15,000 words and examinations. The
course objective is the development of knowledge in the
subject areas and the broader aims of developing skills in
researching and disseminating information in written and
verbal form. Seminar presentation to groups of other
students involved preparation and delivery of a topic using
audio visual techniques and dialogue.

Extra curricular activities: Member of the Students' Union
rock climbing club, travelled on climbing trips to
Switzerland and to Italy. Participated in 'Rag Week'
activities to raise funds for local charities.

(year)–(year)   Redruth Comprehensive School,
Crawford.

Qualifications: A levels: English (B), History (A),
                Economics (B).
                GCSEs: English (B), Mathematics (B),
                History (A), French (C), Physics (C),
                Chemistry (C).

(Continued)

Positions of responsibility: School monitor. Junior
secretary of school Outdoor Pursuits Club. Assistant in
school Youth Club.

Career plans: Having successfully completed a degree
course I am now ready to enter employment. I feel that I
am suited to any post requiring an organised and
methodical approach. I am flexible and prepared to follow
any course of vocational training, and I recently enrolled
at evening classes to learn basic keyboard and computing
skills.

Additional information: Hold a full clean driving licence.
Have travelled abroad and speak everyday French. My
degree studies required working to deadlines, organising a
personal timetable, managing resources and liaising with
other students and academic staff, skills which I am sure
will be valuable in employment.

References: Dr Julie Anderson, Department of History,
The University of North Yorkshire, Leeds.

CURRICULUM VITAE

Sarah Charlotte King   **Age:** 30
122 Peterson Avenue   **Marital status:** married
Manston   **Health:** excellent
Warburton   **Nationality:** British
W17 6RQ
Tel: (01776) 884302

Profile: Experienced waitress with City and Guilds
certificate in Food Hygiene procedures. Competent with
tills, cash handling, customer care and all catering duties.
Smart appearance, good communication skills and
excellent punctuality and reliability. Married with two
children, arrangements have already been made to cover
child care for the youngest child to facilitate my return to
employment.

Employment experience:
(year)–(year): Waitress and bar person, the Old Toad
Hotel and Restaurant, Warburton. Duties included bar
work, cash handling, serving meals, taking orders from
diners in the restaurant, serving, being polite and sociable
with diners. Reason for leaving: left to start a family.

(year)–(year): Silver Service Waitress, the Stag's Head,
Oldcotes, Warburton.
Duties as above with addition of silver service waitressing,
helping with bookings, preparing snacks and starters when
required.

(Continued)

(year)–(year): Waitress, Sally's Dining Rooms, Staithes, Warburton.
Duties included serving customers, taking orders, some till work, food preparation and ensuring a very high standard of service in the restaurant.

Training: (year)–(year) Somerton College of Further Education. City and Guilds certificate in Food Hygiene, college certificate in waitressing skills. Achieved distinctions in both courses.

(Year)–(year) Women into Work Course, Warburton Tertiary College. A course organised by the local TEC to assist women with children return to employment.

Education: (year)–(year) Victoria Girls Secondary Modern School, Warburton.
CSE passes in English, Mathematics, French, Domestic Science and History.

Leisure interests: Swimming, music, cooking, looking after my family.

References: Any previous employer.

CURRICULUM VITAE

Name: Eric John Wilson   **Address:** 65 Jacob Street
                                                    Merton
Age: 38   Leeds L12 5TP

Health: excellent   **Tel:** (0113) 773320

Previous work: Labourer, warehouseman, agricultural worker (seasonal), hod carrier. Physically fit, with no health problems of any kind. Able to do any kind of manual work, used to working out of doors in all weathers, honest and reliable. Have references from all previous employers. Can perform basic DIY tasks and have a basic tool set.

Employment record:
(year)–(year) Labourer, David Stevens Building Ltd. Duties involved all basic manual work on building sites. Made redundant in November (year).
(year)–(year) Farm Labourer, Old Cotes Farm. Basic agricultural work, crop picking by hand, tidying up the farmyard, stone wall building and repair, fence erection.
(year)–(year) Warehouseman, Rontex Ltd. Moving goods by hand barrow, stacking goods safely, keeping delivery yard tidy.
(year)–(year) Unemployed – actively seeking work.
(year)–(year) Labourer, Tyzack Manufacturing. Keeping workplace tidy, moving waste to skips, feeding materials to machinists.

Leisure interests: Snooker, walking, music and socialising.

CURRICULUM VITAE

Name: Michael G Scott   67 The Lawns, Stretford,
Rank: Sergeant   Malthill M13 6RR
Age: 40   Tel: (01873) 552130

Profile

Fully qualified computer technician, hold HND Computer
Studies and Applications certificate. All experience gained
with HM Forces Regular Army. Served for 20 years,
retiring with the rank of sergeant. Used to man-
management and personnel duties, training and
supervision, assessing requirements of specific tasks and
ensuring efficient response. Hold a full clean driving
licence and membership of the Association of Advanced
Motorists.

Service record

(year)–(year) Private with REME stationed in Aldershot,
basic military duties and training to achieve
military standards in computer technician
skills, including the HND Computer Studies.

(year)–(year) Corporal Technician, responsible for bench
repairs to various military electronic/
computing equipment. Re-stationed to
Catterick.

(year)–(year) Sergeant Instructor/Technician, responsible
for training of twenty service personnel.
Responsible for service and repair of
various electronic and computing
equipment, maintaining records, field
repairs.

Achievements
Good Service Award (year).
HM Forces Parachuting Course (year).
Certificate in Training Development (year).
HM Forces Survival Training Exercise, Norway (year).
HM Forces Promotion Examinations (years stated).

Additional information
Married with two children, prepared to re-locate for
employment. Possess excellent communication skills,
punctuality and self-motivation. Prepared to accept any
post in the service/sales of computing equipment or
related products. Enjoy dealing with people, planning and
organising activities and working to deadlines. Member of
the HM Forces Benevolent Association.

Leisure interests
Golf, driving, squash, music (self-taught pianist), fund
raising for HM Forces Benevolent Association.

References
Available from CO REME 3rd Btn.

(An example of an Achievement CV)

CURRICULUM VITAE

Susan Jane Whitehead   453 Cheadle Avenue
Age: 28   Sheffield
Marital Status: single S7 4TF
Health: excellent   (0114) 612190

Profile
Have travelled widely in Europe, holding a variety of jobs
including bar work, retail and clerical. Adaptable, speak
everyday French and German. Successfully organised
employment in France and Germany without assistance.
Hold a full British driving licence and an international
driving licence. Car owner.

Achievements
Route 44 Bistro, Bonn, Germany. Promoted to
manager and increased business by 30%. Organised
refurbishment of the premises single-handedly and
obtained the most competitive quote.

Participated in Volunteer Action Week – events included
a sponsored parachute jump to raise funds for local
charities.

Volunteer tutor/counsellor with Summertime Project –
designed to give under-privileged children a chance to try
outdoor activities not normally available to them. Involved
in various activities and sports, supervision, game playing
and pastoral care.

Attended evening classes to learn German, vehicle
maintenance and City and Guilds 981 Youth Training
Skills certificate.

References

Mrs D Yeomans	Mr C Clarke
67 Vere Crescent	45 Alfreton Avenue
Sheffield	Sheffield
S2 4TY	S12 5RE

Leisure interests
Badminton, swimming, driving and maintaining my car.

Education
(year)–(year) Bankwood Valley Comprehensive School.

Qualifications: O levels: English C, Mathematics B,
French B
A levels: French C, English Literature D

PART FOUR

FIND THE JOB AND
TAILOR YOUR APPLICATION

Where To Look

Vacancies are advertised in newspapers and magazines, professional journals, Job Centres, employment agencies and outside employers' premises. Advertised vacancies are the normal recruitment method although speculative approaches have gained in popularity.

Newspapers and Magazines need to be chosen carefully. There may be a specific journal published for your type of work, or newspapers may specialise in your type of post on specific days. To cut the cost of buying newspapers, identify useful publications and buy the most relevant.

There are three types of newspaper: national, regional and local. Local newspapers contain local vacancies, regional newspapers deal with advertisements from a wider area, perhaps two or three counties. Generally the grade of job is higher in the regional publications. National newspapers deal almost exclusively with professional vacancies, higher management and executive posts, often involving re-location. Some national papers also carry a selection of international vacancies from other EU member countries, and further afield.

Regular visits to a well-stocked library will also cut the need to buy newspapers. If you need to use a professional journal which the library cannot obtain, a polite request to a professional user can sometimes secure a copy, even if it is a little out of date. As a Job Club leader I have often arranged for Job Club members to visit companies' premises to borrow or read trade journals, and generally the response by employers has been very generous.

Take your time when reading advertisements. They are sometimes poorly thought out and are easy to misunderstand. Journals and newspapers are also important for their information. Get into the habit of reading the news columns: look for information about companies which are doing well. Many local and regional publications include a business round-up which covers new developments in the area. By keeping your ear to the ground in this way you can monitor the situation and hear about job opportunities early.

Employment Agencies make their profits from recruitment on behalf of employers. Agencies may be local or national. They operate in three main ways: by advertising vacancies and handling enquiries, by selecting candidates for posts from their registers, and by actively marketing individuals to employers on a speculative basis.

To use agencies you may simply check their advertisements and apply, or you can register yourself with the agency. There should not be any fee for registration or for any other service which the agency offers.

Most agencies deal with a variety of temporary and permanent work. Anyone currently employed will not be interested in temporary work, but for anyone unemployed, temporary work can be a valuable way of building up your CV, gaining references and possibly even permanent employment later.

Before you enter into any temporary work check out the situation with your benefit office. When temporary work finishes, basic Unemployment Benefit or Income Support may be claimed almost immediately, but other payments such as rent allowances, mortgage assistance etc, can take a while to re-start. If you do take temporary work ask your employer for a short letter at the end of the contract stating that your work was temporary and has finished. This may make the renewal of benefits easier.

Employment agencies can be found through telephone directories and press advertisements. Registration is usually a simple matter of filling in a form or submitting a CV and having a short interview with a recruitment manager. Some agencies specialise in particular types of work, others have a broader range of opportunities. National agencies handle vacancies from other parts of the country, and agencies are often inter-linked, so registration with one agency can result in your details being circulated to several sister agencies.

The Internet may be useful to job seekers, especially professional people and those looking for work abroad. Some employers advertise posts in a variety of media, and use of the Internet for this is increasing. It may be viewed at libraries, Cybercafes, or on personal computers.

Word-of-Mouth is a very effective way of finding work, particularly the 'hidden' vacancies which may not be advertised. I know from personal experience how effective word-of-mouth can be, because I once obtained a job in just this way. Also, in some occupational areas, word-of-mouth recruitment is the main way to get new staff. The 'grapevine' is still common.

Network Your Grapevine

You need to set up a network of useful people whom you can contact, on a regular basis, to see if they have heard of any jobs coming up. Your network could include neighbours, relatives, ex-employers, ex-workmates, Employment Services staff: anyone who can offer help. It is important that you contact them regularly (at a time convenient to them), and that you stick to these arrangements. It's also a good idea to let your grapevine members have some details about you, preferably in the form of a CV. Then if a post comes up at short notice they can give their employer, or their contact, your details.

To help you maintain your grapevine network, figure 1 is an example record sheet which you can draw up and fill in with reminders about how and when to contact people. Remember – you never get anything without asking! If you approach people, in a polite manner, without being over-bearing, they will often help you in your job search. My experience as a Job Club leader is that it is the people who operate a grapevine who get the jobs!

Network Chart

CONTACT: David Jenkins at Coldwell Logistics, tel: 640210
BECAUSE: He is Personnel Officer
TIMES: 1–2 pm or 4–4.30 pm Wednesday or Thursday

CONTACT: Susan Hastings at Smith's Cleaners,
         45, The Square
BECAUSE: Susan works in administration and types up any
         vacancies
TIMES: Any lunch time 12–1 pm, except Friday

CONTACT: Mr Holmes, Proprietor, Cheswick Domestic
         Services, tel: 945219
BECAUSE: Mr Holmes is expecting a new contract in the
         next few weeks and will need extra staff,
         possibly on a permanent basis
TIMES: After 5 pm any week day, or after 3 pm
         Saturday, once weekly, for six weeks from
         (date)

CONTACT: Stephen Green, at Pole Star Employment
         Agency, tel: 672319
BECAUSE: He handles your registration and he is marketing
         you to employers
TIMES: Preferably early morning any week day

Figure 1.

Have A Systematic Plan

Record keeping is vital when you are looking for work, especially when you are making speculative approaches to employers. It lets you see at a glance how many applications you have made and helps you to keep up your level of activity. Watch any applications still pending, monitor your progress and identify any weak points in your campaign. Figure 2 gives a suggested design for a record sheet which you can use or adapt.

DATE	COMPANY DETAILS	CONTACT NAME	JOB TITLE	METHOD OF APPLICATION	RESULT

Figure 2

A timetable is important, especially if you are currently unemployed. A regular routine enables you to make efficient use of your time. Get into the habit of completing pre-planned tasks, in order to re-motivate yourself and to keep up your activity level.

As a Job Club leader I often meet people who fail because they are disorganised: the newspaper advertisement they missed because they didn't read that week's edition; the application form they really meant to fill in but never completed; the job they missed because they forgot to contact their grapevine network. An organised routine is vital.

A useful way to organise your activities is a series of work sheets, listing your regular tasks and any urgent things which need to be done. A weekly or daily system could be used, depending on the intensity of your job search and the time you have available.

Standard tasks such as reading a particularly useful newspaper, recording any information found there, contacting people at a pre-arranged time, ringing the employment agency, getting more photocopies of your CV; all these could be listed and checked off as you complete them.

Here is a work sheet which you may copy or adapt to help you organise your regular routines.

Day	Activity	Check
MONDAY	Visit Job Centre	
	Copy more CVs	
	Read weekend newspapers for advertisements	
	Respond to any suitable ads	
	Contact Employment Agency	
TUESDAY	Telephone Dave Browitt and Susan White	
	Visit business library	
	Any other business	

Day	Activity	Check
WEDNESDAY	Speculative approaches	
	Check Job Centre	
THURSDAY	Attend WP course at college	
	Sign on for benefit	
	Check local paper for vacancies	
FRIDAY	Read regional press for adverts	
	Respond to any suitable vacancies	
	Check Job Centre	
SATURDAY	Phone Aunt Susan: have any jobs come up at her company?	
	Buy more stationery	
SUNDAY	Go swimming	

Advertisements – How To Read Them

Advertisements must be read carefully and more than once, particularly if they are large and detailed. Careful perusal can provide clues about the post on offer, and the kind of person who is wanted. Take time to consider how best to 'slant' your approach.

Adjusting the emphasis of your application to suit a particular advertisement produces a better response. My personal experience as a Job Club leader has taught me that the 'standard approach' often gets knocked out at the first fence. It cannot help being bland. It does not address the vacancy closely enough. Employers seldom interview everyone who applies. The short list consists of people who have made the best approach, not only because they presented their applications well, but because they have made their applications relevant. They included useful information and showed their interest in the job.

So, how do you read an advertisement? The trick is to lift out any useful information about the job or the employer. Close attention to the wording of the advertisement usually indicates the kind of qualities expected. A few examples may make this clearer.

TOPHAMS SUPERMARKETS PLC

require an Assistant Manager for their Leeds branch. Supervisory experience essential, preferably in retail. Numerate, good communicator, smart appearance, age 25 years or over, cash handling, staff motivation and stock handling experience preferred, but will train a suitable applicant. Good starting salary with increments for improved efficiency, company pension scheme and discount on goods.

Applications in writing to:
TOPHAMS PLC
TOPHAM HOUSE
BRIGSWORTH
YORKSHIRE
B5 6TY

What information can we get from this advertisement?

1 The fact that the company is a 'PLC' (Public Limited Company) suggests it is a large concern.
2 'Supervisory experience essential' – they want someone who has controlled staff, and who already has management skills.
3 'Good starting salary with increments' – the company wants a motivated individual, able and willing to make improvements to increase sales and efficiency, willing to chase any bonuses or incentives. They don't want someone who is going to sit back and let the branch tick over and run by itself.

4 'Company pension scheme' – the company is interested
   in the well-being of its staff and they regard the job/
   career as long term.
5 Further details reveal that the suitable candidate should
   be numerate – for balancing tills and accounts work; a
   good communicator – able to deal with other managers,
   members of staff and customers, liaise with outside
   agencies such as Weights and Measures officials, Health
   and Safety inspectors, the Fire Brigade etc; aged 25
   years up – suggesting that most of the staff will be
   younger than 25 and that the candidate will have many
   years left for development within the company. Stock
   handling suggests a candidate with a definite retail
   background.

SUSAN'S DINER – THE PLACE TO EAT!

We require additional crew members for our
friendly fast-food restaurant.

Smart and friendly appearance
with catering experience preferred.

Flexible hours with free taxi home after midnight

AGE: 18 years minimum

LOCATIONS: City Centre and Fordham

CONTACT: Susan Rigby on 01623–521877

1 The restaurant is described as 'fast-food': it is not a traditional restaurant with staff wearing 'black and whites'. It is likely to attract clients from the younger end of the market, and the ages of the staff are likely to reflect this.

2 '18 years minimum' – it is probably a licensed premises.

3 'Smart and friendly appearance' (perhaps fashionable, slightly to the casual side) 'preferably with catering experience'. Attention to cleanliness, length of finger-nails, hair style etc. is important in this kind of job.

4 'Flexible hours' – restaurants of this kind are generally open all day and into the night, and a shift system will operate for the staff. Anyone applying for this post would have to think about the hours that the catering industry often work.

5 Contact: Susan Rigby. Note the informality implied. Also that applications are invited by telephone, not in writing. Reason: personality is important in this kind of work and the employer will be able to judge applicants more accurately on the telephone.

I cannot list every single type of advertisement and its details. What I have tried to do in these examples is to show you how to gain by 'reading between the lines' of an advertisement before replying.

It is very important to develop good reading habits. A common fault is to gloss over advertisements and miss important points. Also some advertisements are badly designed, and require extra careful reading; or they may be small, with lots of fine print detail. Some carry more than one job, perhaps a senior post with a junior post underneath, in smaller print. So the rule is: read carefully!

Researching Employers
This is necessary for applications and for interview preparation. One way is to go to the main library in your district, which holds business information, and find any

information which could be useful. A helpful resource is The Companies' Register, which is compiled by the Government's Department of Trade and Industry. It registers limited companies which have been operating for a minimum of two years. From the Register you can get details about limited companies' performance and activities. The register gives information about the company name; registered office; date of incorporation; and the date of the latest report from the company. The register is usually held on microfiche at libraries.

Business and trade directories, annual reports and yearbooks may also yield information: size, assets, main and subsidiary areas of activity, how long they have been running etc.

Other types of library may be useful too: science and technology libraries, academic libraries and general reference libraries. Unfortunately not all companies can be researched through these avenues; small companies may not be included in trade directories, or may not have a sufficient turnover to have to disclose details in the Companies' Register. You could also telephone the employer (or get a friend to do so) to make enquiries about the company products and services.

If the employer is a public service, such as a shop, restaurant, or a public authority of some kind, then research should be a fairly easy task. With shops or restaurants, simply visit the premises to get some ideas; a visit and a sharp eye should provide the observant job hunter with everything needed! An hour's work on the hoof can mean the difference between success and failure. Needless to say, if an employer sends you any information, perhaps with an application form, then they will expect you to read it closely and use it in your application.

Methods Of Application
Applications can be divided into 2 basic types:

1. Response to advertised vacancies.
2. Speculative approaches.

Applications may be by letter and CV, by telephone, by personal visit or by application form. Depending on the type of job you want you might find that one particular method of application is preferred. Advertisements for clerical posts often request a hand written letter to show presentation skills; jobs with a lot of personal contact with people may prefer a phone call in the first instance.

Preparation is the key to success. Poorly thought out applications get filed in the bin! So, before you put pen to paper or pick up the telephone, think a little about what you wish to say for yourself, your best points and relevant skills or the experience you have to offer.

How To Apply
Letters
Presentation is important when you are writing letters to employers. Your letter and CV are the first point of contact between you and the employer who has nothing else to go on. A letter which is poorly set out, crumpled, has spelling mistakes and alterations is unlikely to impress.

DO:

Use plain white writing paper (size A4 is standard for business letters).

Use a guide sheet to get straight lines.

Use black ink or black biro (because the letter may be photocopied by the employer and black ink gives the best copies).

Check that your pen is full and use a pen which suits you.

Write a rough version on scrap paper first. Examine it

critically – does it address the post and the employer properly?

Check your spelling, or preferably get someone else to check it.

Try to get the name of the person to write to, even if an advertisement invites you to write 'to the manager'. It will show motivation if you telephone first and get the name.

End your letter correctly: if you know the person's name, sign it 'yours sincerely'; if you do not have their name, sign it 'yours faithfully'.

Use the correct size of envelope.

Make sure that the address is correctly placed on the envelope and that it is legible. Include a post code when known.

Quote any reference number given in the advertisement.

Keep your letter fairly brief and to the point: your CV will carry most of your details, your letter should draw attention to relevant information. As a general rule, letters should be from one side to a side-and-a-half of A4 paper.

Post it in good time for the closing date.

Keep a copy – you may need to review your application before attending an interview.

DON'T:

Don't use a blotchy pen or a pencil.

Don't type your letters or use a WP. Presentation may improve but it is generally accepted that letters are handwritten and CVs are typed. (Some large companies use handwriting analysis in their selection procedures.)

Don't apologise for anything – you are writing on business.

Don't cross out mistakes or use correction fluid – write the letter again on a fresh sheet of paper.

Don't use a style of written English which you normally wouldn't use. (Verbose or pedantic words and phrases will only thicken your sauce – they won't make it any more tasty! Avoid using a Thesaurus to find words which are rare, under the impression that they will make your letters seem more professional.)

Don't experiment with different layouts – stick to the business layout given in this book.

The following example letter is a sensible design for all job applications. Note that the sender's address is given at the top right hand side, (A), the date is always included below this, (B), then the addressee's details are included on the left hand side, (C), followed by the salutation, (D), then the main body of the letter, (E), followed by the signature and name in block letters, (F).

If you use this layout then you can be sure of producing a professional letter each time. You may notice that when you get replies back from employers they alter the layout to suit their particular letter-head design, moving addresses to the left or to the centre, or mixing layouts together to fit their personalised stationery. For handwritten letters, however, the following example is the best one to use.

(Example Letter Design)

(A)   34 Trent Avenue
      ROTHERHAM
      South Yorkshire
      S40 3WB

(B)   21 March (year)

(C) Mrs R Thompson
    Personnel Officer
    Hague Computers
    45 Yarrow Road
    GOOLE
    Humberside
    G3 5UC

(D) Dear Mrs Thompson

(E) I am writing in response to the advertisement for a
    Trainee Computer Programmer, as published in the
    Yorkshire Chronicle, 18 March (year).

    I have recently completed a BTEC National Certificate in
    Computer Studies at Rotherham Business College and I
    am seeking a post which will allow me to develop my
    computing skills in a business environment. I am a car
    owner and re-location to Goole will not cause any
    inconvenience. I enclose a current CV with details of my
    career and education to date. I feel that I can fulfil all the
    requirements of the post on offer, and I should be
    obliged if you would send further details and an
    application form.

    I shall be available for an interview at any time
    convenient to you and I look forward to hearing from
    you in the near future.

    Yours sincerely

(F)

    TINA D MORGAN

Notice how quickly the applicant draws attention to the title of the post: within two lines the reader knows exactly what the letter is about. This make the letter businesslike and to the point. Few details are given about the applicant since most of her details will be on the enclosed CV.

A positive statement as to her feelings about the job is followed by a definite ending and the correct signing 'Yours sincerely' since she had a named person to address. A concise but relevant introduction by the applicant.

Brevity is often the difference between rejection and further interest. A letter asking for an application form can be very brief, if you wish, simply stating the post which interests you and requesting the application form.

When an advertisement invites you to write with 'full details' of yourself, then the letter may be slightly longer, but the same principles apply. A rambling letter that doesn't get to the point can only lessen your chances. Slanting is important as shown by this example advertisement and two letters written in response to it; one is a 'standard' letter, the second an improved version.

ADVERTISEMENT

The Interior Design Trades Journal requires a talented Features Writer to work on the leading business publication for the Interior Design Industry. We are read by designers, retailers, wholesalers and manufacturers. We keep them informed of new ideas, business trends and developments.

A Features Writer is required to supplement our small team. The preferred applicant will be a competent writer, possibly a journalist with enthusiasm for interior design. The post is based in Reading and excellent re-location facilities are available. We offer excellent salary and fringe benefits, 6 weeks' holiday and business expenses.

Please write with CV to:
MR D RODGERS
PERSONNEL OFFICER
WHITEGATE PUBLICATIONS
123 HENLEY AVENUE
READING R5 1TZ

What information is given in this advertisement?

1 Any form of journalism is likely to involve working to deadlines and to publication dates, so pressure to conform to timetables will be part of the job.
2 'A Competent Writer' is required, but writing skills can involve a variety of different types of journalism.
3 The post is with a 'small team' which indicates the size of the journal's staff. Being part of a small group may require flexibility to fill in for other members of staff.

4 Keyboard skills will be essential.
5 'Enthusiasm for Interior Design' – perhaps someone who is already working in this area, or has experience of interior design, but the advert suggests that anyone with writing skills and motivation could be considered.
6 Responsibility for making a timetable, organising interviews, travel, organisational and administrative skills are all important parts of this post.
7 Ability to write to a 'house style' will be important: the publication is established and obviously successful, so changes are not required in the format and language of the journal. The interviewer will almost certainly expect to see evidence of published work from the applicant.

Replies to Adverts
George Jenkins is forty-two. He is well educated, holds a BA(HONS) degree in Design History and he has written for academic journals, and produced dissertations for his degree. He has also contributed to journals such as 'Furniture Review' and 'House Interior Monthly'. He has a keen interest in furniture, antiques, decor and interior design, and he and his wife have restored and designed their cottage interior. He can drive, and he has worked as a lecturer at a college of Art and Design for most of his career. He can use a word processor, and he is computer literate. He is now seeking a change from the lecturing career which he began fifteen years ago, and he feels that he could make a living as a full-time technical writer, and the post with the Interior Design Trade Journal interests him.

So, how should George go about his application? He has relevant experience, he has writing skills and some part-time journalistic experience. He teaches on Interior Design courses, has an excellent knowledge of the subject area, and he reads constantly and is aware of the current state of affairs in interior design. On the following page you can see George's letter of application, followed by some critical notes.

45 Raeburn Drive
YORK
Y13 8VO

10 June (year)

Mr D Rodgers
Personnel Officer
Whitegate Business Publications
123 Henley Avenue
READING
R5 1TZ

Dear Mr Rodgers

I am a graduate in Design History, currently looking for work
in journalism. I hold a BA(HONS) degree and I have written
articles for various academic journals, on subjects such as
Economic History and Population Trends in Victorian
Britain, and I have written for some furniture and home
decor magazines. I have also done some research work and
information processing.

I have worked as a lecturer for the last fifteen years, but I
now wish to change direction and enter journalism. I feel
that I have achieved as much as I can in lecturing, and that a
change of scene would be a good idea. I have not read your
particular journal, but I am sure that I could fit into your
existing team efficiently. I notice that you are advertising a
post as a Features Writer for your trade journal, and I should
be obliged if you would consider my application further. I
feel that I have relevant skills which would be useful in
technical journalism.

I enclose a CV and I look forward to hearing from you in the
near future.

Yours sincerely

GEORGE JENKINS BA(HONS)

This letter lacks any real meat. The applicant uses vague terms, the letter is slow to state the post applied for, and much of it is taken up with irrelevant details of academic work, rather than what he has had published.

Stating that he has never heard of the Interior Design Trades Journal is bad, and his desire to change direction from an established career for 'a change of scene' is weak.

Little is done to sell the applicant. It is possible that the CV may shed more light on the applicant's potential, but for a post in written communication a well-written application is vital.

So, unfortunately, George has not made use of his experience and writing skills. His letter is bland and does not read well, with minimal thought to content and leading the reader's eye to relevant details.

Here is an improved version, with better use of his experience and clearer information. The second version is a little longer, but still gets the information across in a well-presented manner without rambling on.

45 Raeburn Drive
YORK
Y13 8VO

10 June (year)

Mr D Rodgers
Personnel Officer
Whitegate Business Publications
123 Henley Avenue
READING
R5 1TZ

RE: POST OF FEATURES WRITER

Dear Mr Rodgers

I am writing in response to your advertisement for the above post.

I am a Design History graduate and lecturer, with published academic works and articles for journals such as 'The

Furniture Review' and 'House Interior Monthly'. My wife and I restored our nineteenth century cottage and completely designed the interior, and I have a keen interest in all aspects of interior design.

I am interested in changing career and entering full-time journalism in this field, having enjoyed the challenge of part-time writing and gaining personal satisfaction from practical work on our home. I have excellent communication skills, a full clean driving licence and I am able to liaise with people from a wide variety of backgrounds. I am also computer literate.

In my academic work I have used a variety of research techniques, including interviews, visits and questionnaires. I am currently in charge of my department's examination administration, a task which involves organisation and working to strict deadlines.

I can alter my writing style to suit any particular journal and I include examples of my published work. Re-location to Reading will not pose any problem, and I am confident that I can become a useful member of your team.

I enclose a CV and I look forward to meeting you to discuss this exciting post.

Yours sincerely

GEORGE JENKINS

The second version is much improved. It quotes relevant skills and experience and is slanted correctly. It also emphasises George's ability to work under pressure and gives proper reasons for changing career. It includes details of the journals he has written for and examples of his work.

An application letter should split into 3 sections:

1 The introduction – state quickly the reason for the letter, and the title or reference number of the post.
2 The 'sales pitch' – give relevant information and draw attention to your most relevant skills and abilities.
3 The end – finish in a purposeful manner, and state that you are available for an interview at any convenient time.

Here are some more example letters to advertised vacancies for various jobs. They follow the guidelines and should give you a good basis on which to model your own.

65 Whiteways Road
Carrfield
PRESTON
P4 8EL

9 February (year)

Mr R Greaves
Recruitment Manager
Greenups Transport Ltd
Unit 6
Redgrove Industrial Estate
PRESTON
P14 8RG

Dear Mr Greaves

I am writing in response to your advertisement for an
Assistant Transport Manager, as published in Freight and
Haulage Weekly, and I should like to offer my application.

I have 7 years' experience in transport management,
gained with two employers. I am used to planning routes,
tachograph systems, record keeping, transport law and
vehicle maintenance. I have been responsible for up to
thirty drivers and vehicles and in my last post I was
temporarily in charge of all operations in the owner's
absence. I hold a class 2 HGV licence and a full clean car
licence.

Having recently been made redundant, I am now seeking
a similar post elsewhere in the haulage and transport
industry.

I enclose a CV with full details of my career and details of
my previous employers, and I look forward to meeting you
to discuss my application.

Yours sincerely

GARY H KING

23 Prince Street
THORNCLIFFE
T4 9WP
(01674) 348819

4 March (year)

Mrs C Bannister
Director
Alpha Marketing
Victoria Buildings
Market Street
WHISTON
W2 6VO

Dear Mrs Bannister

I note with interest the advertisement for a Marketing Assistant with your company, published in the County Gazette, 2 March (year).

I would like to be considered for the post and I should be obliged if you could peruse my enclosed CV.

As you can see, I have 5 months' experience of marketing, gained with Pole Star Enterprises. This included direct research by questionnaires, interviews and sampling. I am used to writing reports, designing pictograms and disseminating information for use by colleagues or clients. I am currently studying for the Diploma in Marketing by correspondence course, which I am financing myself. I hold a full clean driving licence.

Although I realise that I do not have the experience which you stated in your advertisement, I feel that I am capable of developing quickly and becoming a useful member of your marketing staff.

I would appreciate the opportunity to meet you to discuss the post, and I am available at any time you find convenient.

Yours sincerely

MISS JANE HAWKSWORTH

Telephone Calls

The telephone has many advantages for the job seeker: it is quicker than writing letters, you can get an immediate response and telephone conversation is flexible. Once in contact with the employer you can enquire about any other vacancies available, if they would hold your details on file, or if any other branches of their organisation might be recruiting. You can't do this in writing as your letter would become over long and lack focus. One disadvantage with the telephone, however, is that calls can be forgotten, and the employer does not have anything to file.

Telephone calls, like letters, can be made in response to advertisements, or they may be speculative. For advertised vacancies which ask you to telephone, many of the points covered in the section on letter writing remain valid: read the advertisement carefully; look for useful information; think about what *you* have to offer and how to present it in the best way.

Make a few notes before you pick up the phone. The telephone is more direct than a letter: once speaking with an employer you cannot really back out of the application – you have to be ready and confident when you start. With letters you can edit and re-write your letter before sending it off, and no-one will be any the wiser. But the telephone allows no such luxury, so preparation is essential.

Here are the secrets of using the telephone. Some apply only to calls in response to advertisements, others may apply to speculative approaches as well.

1 Prior to calling:
  Read the advertisement carefully – why do they want you to telephone?
  Are they going to test your telephone manner? Or is the job one where personality is important?
  What kind of skills are they looking for? Look for clues about the company and the post, make a list of what you feel you have to offer.

If there is a reference number quote it in your call.
Write down the questions you want to ask and take the list to the telephone.

2 On the telephone:
Have the advertisement with you.
Have your CV with you.
Is there a specific person or department whom you have to contact?
Introduce yourself by name. State clearly for which post you are applying.
Speak clearly; don't gabble your name and address.
Be prepared to talk about yourself, what you feel you have to offer, your experience, why you are applying.
Ask any questions in a positive manner.
Check back through any interview arrangements: times and locations. (Unless the location is particularly difficult to find don't ask the employer for details – any applicant should be able to sort out this themselves. If the location is very difficult most employers will offer directions.)
Thank them for their time and attention.

Work through these preparation ideas even if you only want to order an application form and further details by telephone. Often applicants are caught out when asked questions for which they are not ready.

Answering Machines
Many people find answering machines difficult. These are increasingly common. Small employers have them because they may be out of the office frequently, and large employers may use a 24-hour answering machine to handle applications for an advertised vacancy. Have a written script ready with you by the telephone, which you can read out if the situation requires.

The script should include your name and address, the job title or reference number of the post, and either a request for an application form or that the employer contact you. Remember to speak slowly and clearly when quoting your name and address and telephone number. Don't hang up and ring back later, hoping to get a personal response. By the time you get a personal response the employer may have collected enough names and addresses from the answering machine and may not accept any more applicants.

Try to make your calls on a phone which is situated somewhere quiet. Nothing gives a worse impression than a lot of background noise, especially if it sounds like a crowded room in a public house! If you don't have a telephone of your own ask friends if they would mind if you used theirs to make some applications. Offer to pay, of course. Alternatively find a well-situated public call box, and make sure that you have plenty of change or use a phone card. If you're unemployed and eligible then join a Job Club, where you will have access to free telephones as well as other facilities.

One way to improve your telephone technique is to script the opening of your call. Just a few opening lines on a sheet of paper can help you overcome the initial hurdle. This technique is a great success with members of my Job Clubs who are nervous of the telephone. If you feel that you are not very good on the telephone then try some role play, talking over the lines of your script, or ask a friend to role play an employer with you. Your telephone skills will quickly improve.

Remember, employers will not expect a perfect telephone call. The occasional mistake does not automatically rule out the chance of an interview.

Application Forms
Application forms are common in selection procedures. Employers often issue application forms and supporting information rather than request letters and accompanying CVs. There are a number of reasons:

1 The company design their own application form and they know what kind of information they want. A CV, although well designed and informative, may not include this particular information.
2 Employers can read the application form very quickly because it splits up information efficiently and they know where to look for specific items. On a CV these would be laid out differently and would take longer to find.
3 Theoretically it is fairer to all applicants as everyone fills in the same form and has an equal chance.
4 Applications are kept to a sensible working length.
5 The application form is a legally binding document – there is a clause stating that the information you have supplied is true and accurate to the best of your knowledge. Any offer of employment is based upon this being checked and validated.

Application forms have their pros and cons. On one hand a lot of work is done for us; we don't have to consider layout and design. All we need to do is follow the instructions correctly, fill the form in accurately and return it in good time. On the other hand application forms often don't have much room for detailed answers; information has to be short, and the form often 'directs' your answer, with little space to 'slant' your approach.

However, most application forms do include 'general questions', usually towards the end of the form. These questions follow various styles: 'What do you feel you can offer this post?' or, 'Give details of your background, leisure interests or any other information which could contribute to this company' or, 'What made you apply for this position?' Examples such as these can all be found on modern application forms. They offer you the chance to add some individual slant to your application.

Completing an application form is simple:

1 Read through the whole form carefully. Make sure that

you understand all the questions, watch out for overlap from one page to another, where similar information is required for different questions, eg Education and Further Education.

2 Read all the instructions carefully. Make sure you know which instructions apply to which questions. The instructions are usually found at the top of the first page, but special instructions may be located near specific questions, or perhaps may be included in the supporting information supplied with the application form. The employer will mark application forms on neatness, presentation and also on accuracy when following instructions.

3 Take a photocopy of the form and write your answers on the copy. This will give you practice writing your answers, and will enable you to check that your answer can fit into the space. Pay particular attention to the general questions, and use your CV as a prompt list for the simpler questions.

4 Take your time when you transfer information to the proper form. Try to split it into sections, do a section and then have a short rest before moving on to another.

5 Presentation is important: use a good pen with black ink. Only type out your answers if the form gives permission in the instructions, and keep your form clean and tidy.

6 Answer all the questions that apply to you. If any questions do not apply, either put a *neat* line through the space given, or write 'N/A' (not applicable). This shows that you have seen the question, and tells the employer that you have not missed it through carelessness or avoided it through reluctance to answer. Never, unless given permission, include your CV with an application form and put 'see CV' as an answer.

7 Check the form thoroughly, take a copy for reference, sign and date it, and return it in good time for the closing date.

If you follow these ideas then you should have little difficulty completing application forms correctly.

Sometimes employers present you with an application form to complete whilst you are waiting for your interview. There may be a time limit which you must observe. Nevertheless, it is still a good idea to flick quickly through it to read the questions and the instructions to check if any do not apply to you. You should also take your CV to interviews, then if you meet this situation, you have your prompt list handy to help you fill in the form.

If you have problems filling in application forms, practise on blank ones. Do exercises using block capital printing. Many forms require block capitals as presentation is neater. Also, as most people's handwriting is bigger than their printing, you can get more information onto an application form if answers are printed.

Speculative Approaches
The speculative approach to employers is increasingly popular and often succesful. The idea is that rather than simply respond to advertisements, you actively market yourself to employers by letter, telephone or personal visit.

Choosing target companies for speculative approaches could be done simply by taking names and addresses out of telephone directories, business directories, or trade journals. But it is better if you know that the company is in a position to offer employment: they have recently won a new contract, they are expanding or they have announced higher profits for last year's trading. The objective of all speculative approaches is the same: to get your name on file for any posts which may arise in the near future. The advantage, to the employer, of a speculative approach is that they might fill a vacancy without having to spend any advertising fees (expensive and not always successful) and it saves all that sifting through applications. The advantage to the job seeker is that a speculative approach may face no competition. An element of luck does come into it – your speculative application might reach an employer's desk at just the right time. But in any case, many employers will hold individuals' details in 'skills pools' until a suitable vacancy occurs.

Because there is no information from an advertisement to work on, research for speculative applications is essential. It's no use applying to an employer, telling them how useful you could be in their organisation, and how you could fit into their activities, if they don't use your particular type of skills and abilities. You need to discover what service they offer, what products they make, how big they are, whom you need to contact (not always a personnel officer) and make sure that you find out that person's name. Don't hesitate to telephone the company to ask on this point! This shows that you are motivated and enthusiastic.

Provided that this preparation has been done, impress-ive results can be achieved through speculative appli-cations. Obviously some might land on stony ground, but an encouraging statistic is that over half of the people who have got jobs through my Job Clubs have done so by speculative applications.

The Speculative Letter
This requires many of the same techniques needed for replies to advertisements. Some people include a stamped addressed envelope with their speculative letters, but I think that is unnecessary. My experience shows many employers will respond of their own accord. If they do not reply this does not mean that they have ignored your application – some employers file speculative applications and only contact the applicant when a suitable post arises. If you wish you might follow up your speculative letter with a telephone call if you have not heard from the employer.

Here are some good example letters:

23 Green Lane
SHEFFIELD
S7 4BV

3 January (year)

Mr E W Vickers
Personnel Manager
Orion Hotel
The Square
SHEFFIELD
S1 3TG

Dear Mr Vickers

I recently read in the local press that the planned extension of the Orion Hotel is going ahead and that it will open in April of this year.

I feel confident that the extension will further increase the business of the Orion Hotel, and I wonder if you might require extra staff to cater for the increased number of guests and clients.

I would like to offer my experience in the hotel trade to your company, and I should be obliged if you would consider my enclosed CV. I have over ten years' experience in hotel work, including four years as an assistant manager of a small hotel in Devon. I have passed Part I of the Hotel and Catering Management Examinations, and I am used to customer contact, security procedures, Fire Prevention, Health and Safety regulations and staff supervision. I can supply references as required. I am a non-smoker and I hold a clean driving licence.

I would be pleased to attend an interview at any time suitable to yourself should any vacancy be available. If there are no vacancies at present, would you hold my details on file in case any arise in the near future?

I wish you every success in the coming year at the Orion Hotel and I look forward to hearing from you soon.

Yours sincerely

FREDERICK T YEOMANS

45 Smithy Crescent
LOUGHBOROUGH
L19 8WN
(01509) 451190

13 June (year)

Mrs T Johnson
Proprietor
The Moonshadow Café
White Road
LOUGHBOROUGH
L2 4VZ

Dear Mrs Johnson

I noticed that you have recently refurbished the interior of the
Moonshadow Café and I wonder if you require any more staff
now that you are open again.

I am an experienced waitress, with my own uniform, and
am of smart, clean and tidy appearance. I can use an
electronic till and I have a pleasant and friendly personality.
I have worked in hotel restaurants, cafés and public houses,
and I have references from all my previous employers.

I would appreciate the opportunity to meet you to discuss any
waitressing posts which may arise. I enclose a CV and I look
forward to hearing from you.

Yours sincerely

CHRISTINE R MELVILLE

67 Middle Hay Avenue
REDTOWN
South Yorkshire
R19 5FG

2 March (year)

Mr W A Rodgers
Managing Director
Rodgers Music Shops Ltd
The Civic Centre
DONCASTER
D3 7WW

Dear Mr Rodgers

I am writing to enquire if you have a vacancy for a sales person within any of your company's branches in Doncaster, Sheffield or Chesterfield.

I have five years' retail experience, gained with Stokes Universal Stores, in a variety of departments including furniture, mensware, electronic games, computers and musical keyboards. I am used to cash handling, till operation, stock control and customer care. I adapt easily to new situations and I have excellent communication skills.

In my spare time I am a keen organist, playing regularly at my local church, and I also give private lessons to children. I can sight read and I also have a good knowledge of guitars, pianos and accessories.

If you anticipate a vacancy for which I could be considered I am available for an interview at very short notice and I should be obliged if you would hold my details on file. I enclose my CV and I thank you for your time and attention.

Yours sincerely

JAMES LAWRENCE

The Speculative Telephone Call

A speculative phone call may need one or two preparatory calls first, to find out the name of the person you need to speak to, and then to find out if they are available or the most convenient time to contact them. It is very important to speak to the correct person – someone who can make a decision about interviews and talk to you about any possible vacancies. It's no use talking for twenty minutes to a secretary who can only put an application form in the post. That isn't what you want: you want to visit them and talk to the person who deals with recruitment.

Occasionally you will get rebuffed from speculative telephone calls – the employer cannot spare any time to see you and they do not anticipate any vacancies. Always be polite and thank them for their time. Ask if they know of any other company who might be recruiting at the moment? Would they accept a letter and a CV from you, to file should any jobs come up?

The worst thing that they could say is no – but often if you ask in a polite manner then people will go out of their way to help.

Visits

Speculative visits are also a useful tactic. Apart from asking about any vacancies, the visit can also be used to build contact with employers for the future. Most people pay attention to visitors who enquire about vacancies in person. In some occupations this is the normal way of finding work – the building trade relies heavily on speculative visits. Certain types of employer, however, may not appreciate unsolicited visits: banks, building societies and security companies would be typical examples. But shops, restaurants, warehouse units and factories are all sensible targets.

Call during normal business hours, but always be prepared that they may be busy. Take a few CVs to leave if the manager is not available, and also a pen and paper. Dress appropriately for the type of company and try to choose employers who are situated close together. A good example would be an industrial estate or trading park, or a shopping mall. Visiting gets your name in circulation and builds useful contacts for your grapevine.

PART FIVE

THE INTERVIEW –
YOUR BIG OPPORTUNITY

Interviews are perhaps the easy stage of the application process. A lot of the spadework has now been done.

Always look at an interview as a positive event. Employers never interview anyone unless they feel that person has something to offer – they don't waste time and resources arranging interviews for the sake of it. So when you are invited to an interview, from an advertised vacancy or a speculative approach, think positively.

An interview is a two-way meeting between applicant and employer. It is a conversation and an assessment. The difference between a normal conversation and an interview is that the latter is planned in advance. Employers will list topics and questions to raise; they always prepare for an interview, and so should you. Interviews are for both parties and you should use them to your advantage. Careful planning will develop good interview techniques and get better results.

Employers are impressed by applicants who are prepared for their meeting and who seem happy and confident. For employers, interviews are their opportunity to assess your specific suitability for the post, and to probe your abilities on a more general level: your ability to fit in with the existing members of the workforce, your personality, appearance and attitudes. We judge other people by these factors – how they 'come across' – every day of our lives. Interviewers use personal contact to judge our attitudes, abilities and probable conduct.

Imagine that you were to rent out a room in your house to a lodger. If you advertised in a newspaper and someone telephoned you and said: "My name is Joe Green, I can pay the rent regularly, I'll be a good lodger and I'll take the room" would you tell him to move in and give him a key straight away? Of course you wouldn't! You would invite him round to look at the room, and meanwhile you would be looking at him, his appearance and how he 'came across' to you. You might ask where he had lived before, and could he supply a reference from a previous landlord.

Interviews are very similar. The employer is considering your entry to his 'house', and will assess you on similar lines. Although interviews are not foolproof, they are a fairly accurate way of assessing applicants, and in the hands of a trained interviewer can be very accurate indeed.

Preparation

You may already have researched the employer, but if not, you need to find out lots of relevant information, as discussed on page 71.

You must make plans so that you arrive punctually, dressed smartly. Consider what you wish to say about yourself. Anticipate the main questions you are likely to be asked and practise your answers (especially on any topics which you find difficult to talk about). Also think of a few sensible questions to ask.

Before the Interview

1 Make sure that you know where you are going! An obvious point but one which often puts people in a tight spot. You may think you know the way to the employers' premises, but always check the exact location, travel arrangements, parking, fares, particular traffic problems,

etc. If you can afford the time and money, do a 'dry run' before the interview, so that you can identify any difficulties and plan accordingly. It will not give a good impression if you rush into an interview at the last minute looking as if you have just finished a marathon. It suggests bad planning.

Be especially careful when attending interviews in other cities. Planning has to be tighter, and a dry run may not be feasible because of the costs. Try to see a copy of the local street guide (available in most big libraries). If you are going by public transport check routes and timetables. British Rail and many larger bus and coach operators offer a free planning service to telephone enquirers. If you are unemployed enquire at a Job Centre about the Travel to Interview Scheme.

2 Be punctual. Leave yourself plenty of time to find the right office once you have arrived at the building.

3 Consider your appearance and dress carefully. Dress smartly for interviews: men should wear a suit and tie, a jacket and smart trousers or other formal outfit; women should wear a sensible outfit, with a skirt rather than trousers. It is not always necessary for women to wear a suit, but an interview outfit should reflect the importance of the occasion. In either case, avoid extra bright colours, make sure that your hair is neat, that your shoes are polished and that your clothes are pressed. Even if your outfit is old, pressing and brushing it will make it look better.

Some people do dress casually and still succeed in their interviews, but if you look as if you've just come from painting your house or doing a job underneath your car, then the employer is unlikely to be impressed. First impressions are vital. Show the employer that the interview is important to you and you will emphasise the seriousness of your application.

If you have no smart clothes, get some. If you cannot

afford to buy new clothes then look in second-hand shops. Really good second-hand outfits can be picked up from Oxfam Shops and Overseas Aid Shops quite cheaply. The clothes are cleaned and pressed before being put on sale. Some open-air markets sell 'seconds' from well known chain stores and clothing suppliers, and good bargains can be found by hunting around.

Men should be freshly shaved or their beards/moustaches neatly trimmed. Ladies must think about their make-up: too much can be off-putting, and as with bright coloured clothing it is best to try to avoid startling make-up effects. The only exception would be a job where use of make-up is expected, such as in cosmetic sales or in reception work, but even in these jobs a very individual appearance may be discouraged.

4 Think about the weather when you decide what to wear for an interview. Don't set off in your best outfit, only to get caught out in a sudden rainstorm without an umbrella and finish up thoroughly soaked when you arrive at the interview. On the other hand, wearing a heavy overcoat or jacket and walking some distance to the employer's premises, and finding that their building is overheated, can be equally unfortunate. If this happens take off your coat. Personal comfort is important in an interview. If you feel uncomfortable you will not relax nor be effective.

5 Things to take with you: 2 copies of your CV, pen and paper, any relevant certificates, written references, driving licence (if applicable), a comb, tissues and make-up, as necessary.

6 Write down the questions you wish to ask the employer and take them into the interview with you. If the topics you were going to raise are covered during the interview, rather than say that you don't have any questions to ask, you can show that you had a few points written down. This will show the employer that you prepared for the

interview and that you are keen and motivated. It is also a polite way of paying a compliment to the interviewer, implying that he thought of everything you might want to ask. Acceptable topics to ask about include pay arrangements, induction courses, uniforms, expenses, social activities, and staff restaurant facilities.

Other topics, if applicable, could be development or promotion opportunities, performance review procedures or where the post lies in the organisation of the company. It all varies according to the type of job and the size of the organisation concerned. Research will give you some idea about the type of opportunities on offer with the company. If you can put in a relevant question on a topic which the employer feels is an important part of their operations or procedures, it can earn you bonus points. Always be positive – don't ask about things like sickness arrangements, or grievance procedures within the company.

7 Anticipate the interviewer's questions and think how you would answer them. Interviews are often quite predictable. Once you have attended a few you will find that similar questions come up, in varying forms, time and time again.

8 Try to get an early night before the interview. Do not drink the night before an interview, no matter how relaxed it may make you feel. It will show on you the next day. How would you feel if you prepared for an interview and arrived to find the employer looked 'hung-over' from the night before? Would you feel that you were being given serious consideration? Never go for 'Dutch courage' before an interview for the same reasons.

Conducting The Interview
Good communication between candidate and interviewer(s) is vital and you should try to foster a good relationship with your interviewer right from the start.

From then on, make sure that you conduct yourself properly and make effective use of the meeting.

It has been said that interviewers make up their mind about an applicant within the first 5 minutes. If their conclusion is good, they spend the rest of the interview seeking evidence to support it; if their opinion is negative, they spend the rest of the interview looking for evidence for that!

While this may not be completely true, it highlights the importance of first impressions and the need to communicate well, early.

One way to bridge the gap between you and your interviewer is to use positive body language. This is the system of signals which form an important part of human communications: a series of subtle messages conveyed by movement, posture, eye contact and facial expression. Good body language reinforces your positive points and makes the employer warm to you and form a good opinion.

Poor body language builds a barrier very quickly, stops effective communication and results in failure at interview. Some postures or actions convey specific meanings, and if these are out of context then communication can be adversely affected.

For instance, sitting with your arms folded can be interpreted as saying that you are in charge, and that you don't accept the interviewer's authority, or that you need a barrier between you and them, to protect you or to hide something. None of these interpretations is likely to impress.

Think back to any situations you have encountered where people used incorrect or even threatening body language to you – everyone comes across these situations from time to time. How did you feel? Did you find it easy to deal with them or not? Did you get what you wanted from them? The answer is probably not! The problem is exactly the same for an interviewer.

Many nervous people withdraw into their private space,

retreating from contact with other people, especially when under pressure. On the other hand aggressive people sometimes 'invade' others' private space, perhaps leaning too far forward across the interviewer's desk, or standing too close. The effect can by very off-putting.

The interviewer will interpret your body language and draw conclusions from it. He will look for feedback signals from the applicant. Nodding and smiling, posture and eye contact are important listening skills which show that you are paying attention. The lack of these feedback signals soon causes irritation or negative feelings. Try talking to someone for a while who isn't listening to you and you'll soon get the idea!

Here are a few rules to follow which will help you portray positive body language: you can remember them by the abbrevation P.R.A.S.E.L.

P = Posture – adopt an open posture. Don't fold your arms, bend your head, or adopt a posture which is defensive or aggressive.

R = Relax – this will show the interviewer that you are confident.

A = Avoid unnecessary gestures.

S = Sit facing the interviewer whenever possible.

E = Eye-contact – look at the interviewer, don't let your gaze wander around the room. But don't stare unwaveringly into his eyes.

L = Lean forward *slightly* to show your interest in what the interviewer is saying. You might also lean forward slightly more when you wish to take temporary control, perhaps to ask a question.

Conduct At Interview

1 Look positive and keen, even when you are sitting in the waiting room. Don't look as if this is just one more interview in a string of others. The receptionist or other members of staff may be watching to judge your attitude

and report back to their employer.

2 Respond to any greetings. If they say 'Good Morning' reply in the same way; if they wish to shake hands – shake hands; if they're Eskimos – rub noses!

3 Wait to be invited before sitting down.

4 Look interested and alert at all times. Nod and smile occasionally. These listening skills will show that you are paying attention to the interviewer.

5 Keep a good posture, whether sitting or standing.

6 Speak clearly and don't put your hand in front of your mouth. There's no need to put on an interview voice, just be yourself. Make sure that you can be heard and understood.

7 Don't give lots of 'yes' and 'no' answers. The interview is your chance to sell yourself to the employer, so make use of the opportunity. Don't be passive and expect the interviewer to draw information from you. He might conclude that you are not really interested in the job, that you are a poor communicator or that you are reluctant to discuss areas of your application. None of these conclusions help you. Don't try to take the interview over, but at the same time tell the employer about yourself.

8 Don't be too critical of previous employers or training schemes. The interviewer may wonder if the job or the training scheme was the problem, or was it you? Are you the kind of person who constantly finds fault? This can put an employer off you fairly quickly!

9 Don't chew or eat in an interview. Even if they invite you to have a drink, it is probably best not to, as you may spill it. Some people find that chewing gum or eating a

mint relaxes them, but it simply is not businesslike, and is totally out of place.

10 Ask your questions in a positive manner. This shows confidence. Employers welcome sensible questions. Never ask questions which are not important to you – if the employer asks you why you want to know about this particular point it reflects badly on you if you have no real reason.

11 Always thank the interviewer for his time at the end of the interview. Even if you feel that you have not done very well it is best to go out on a positive note. You might also ask if there is a date by which the employer will tell you the outcome. This will stop you waiting unnecessarily when you could be applying elsewhere. Leave the premises smartly after the interview. Do not loiter around.

Types Of Interview
Interview procedures vary. They may be informal chats in a coffee-room, formal face-to-face situations, a walk around an employer's premises, a panel interview with two or more interviewers, a preliminary interview followed by a second, more selective interview, or a combination of any of these.

A common variation is the Continuation Interview, or the Extension Interview, as some people call it.

This is in two parts: a formal interview with a manager or a personnel officer, followed by a more informal tour and possibly coffee with a junior manager, or perhaps a member of staff. The tour can come first (in which case your formal interviewer will test you to see if you picked up on anything in your tour).

The individual who takes you around the firm, or invites you to have a coffee in the staff lounge, is a member of the interview team. He or she will report back to the formal interviewer and say how they felt about you.

Did you show a lot of enthusiasm and interest? Did you say anything negative? Or let slip any information which you kept from the main interviewer?

Be aware of this technique, and make sure that you wear your 'interview face' at all times. The technique can reveal possible defects such as the applicant who may be very businesslike in a formal interview, but as soon as he is out of the interview room he relaxes and lights up a cigarette and puts up his feet. This could indicate that when the boss is around they work, but when he's not they aren't so busy! Hardly likely to impress a prospective employer!

Panel interviews, where two or more people question and talk to the applicant, tend to be more common in managerial and professional posts. Try to remember each person's name. Don't get flustered by the fact that you have more than one person to talk to. Often you find that only one person will ask the questions; the others might take part at the end and ask a few questions then. If you do have more than one interviewer it may simply be that they represent different sections of the organisation: one interviewer may be from personnel, the other might be a line manager, with direct contact or responsibility for the post. Such interview set-ups are useful for the employer because the personnel officer can interview from the point of long-term potential, the line manager from the short-term objective of doing the job in question.

The panel interview is not insidious; it can be fairer, as the decision to employ is made by two or more people, rather than by one interviewer. Large organisations frequently make use of panels. Many Civil Service posts involve panel interviews. Often an established civil servant is brought onto the interview team from another department, to contribute an impartial opinion.

Remember that, at the end of the day, employers want to take someone on in the post. They cannot keep re-advertising indefinitely, although some employers are very choosy and may interview a large group of people.

THE OBJECT OF THE INTERVIEW IS TO RECRUIT SOMEONE –
MAKE SURE THAT SOMEONE IS YOU!

The kinds of questions asked at an interview depend on the type of job and the policies of the company. Generally, interview questions can be divided into two types: specific job skills and occupational experience, and questions about the applicant's general life skills, and suitability for the post and the company.

Your outlook on life, ambitions, personality, hobbies etc., can all have a bearing on your potential. Your knowledge about the state of affairs in the industry may be probed, and your awareness of current trends, new products or developments assessed.

Your personal situation may also be a topic in the interview. Strictly speaking there are areas which employers are not supposed to ask about, such as child care provision for a working mother, or if a female applicant intends to have any children. These sorts of questions come under the auspices of the Sex Discrimination Act, but questions can be asked in various ways by an employer, and it is not sensible to refuse to answer such questions in your interview. If you prepare sensible answers for these questions then you can avoid any conflict with your interviewer.

Typical Questions
It is impossible to list every question you may meet, but I include a short selection of typical interview questions, with guidelines on how to answer them:

What do you feel you can offer this company?
This kind of question is two-fold: it tests the applicant's self-esteem, and their ability to structure information coherently. A sensible answer would include experience in the field, or in a similar area, ability to adapt to new situations, to learn new skills and procedures, loyalty,

ability to get on with other people.

The answer must show your decisiveness in applying for the post. Be prepared for follow-up questions asking for more details, or for examples of when you have adapted to new situations, what new skills you have learned, or evidence of loyalty.

Tell me what you feel you achieved in your last post.
Again, a test of the applicant's self-esteem. It can also offer an insight into what you see as important to you in your work. Your answer could include successful meeting of deadlines or targets, improvements in procedures, self-development. It is important to say that you have achieved something out of a previous post. Being too negative, or even neutral, could be interpreted as lack of enthusiasm.

Do you have any weaknesses?
The best way to deal with this type of question is to say that you have no weaknesses which would affect your performance in the post on offer. To simply reply that you have no weaknesses at all may sound a little arrogant.

What don't you like about your present post?
A question which can be full of pitfalls! Never find too much to complain about in your present or any previous post (or training course), even if you hated your manager and the job totally.

Try to say that you got something out of it. Be a little philosophical: for example, say that you realise that every job has its own particular problems, and that you feel taking the rough with the smooth is part of every job.

On the other hand your present job must lack something, or you wouldn't be at the interview! So try to balance your answer with a good reason for wanting to move. A sensible answer would concern your career, and the fact that you have taken it as far as possible in your present post. You see a new job as a progressive move. This particular post will offer new challenges and your development will be mutually beneficial to you and your new employer. Alternatively you might use any changes in your domestic situation as a good reason for wanting to move.

What ambitions do you have?
If the post or the organisation offers promotion as a normal part of their activity, then your answer should be positive, with lots of plans for self-improvement and increase in responsibilities and reward. If the post or the organisation does not automatically offer promotion opportunities then a 'the sky's the limit' answer may put the employer off – it might suggest that you would soon become frustrated and want to move on. Here you should slant your answer more to leisure ambitions, a new car, a special holiday: anything to give your answer some detail without making the post seem below you or giving the impression that you will move on quickly.

Remember, the employer almost always wants staff to stay long-term. Recruitment is a costly business. Constant staff and management changes cause disruption in the workforce, reduce production, and may spoil relationships in the workplace.

What level of salary are you looking for?
A question which many people find intimidating. The first point is that you should have some idea of the 'going rate' for the type of posts to which you apply. Monitoring the advertisements and making enquiries with your contacts should indicate the current level of salaries and perks.

You should work out your needs taking into account your living costs, bills, rent/mortgage, life insurance premiums etc, then arrive at a figure around which you can work and negotiate at interviews. Your answer should take into account your value as an employee, and should be progressive, if possible. But a gigantic leap from a low salary to a very high one is unlikely to be achieved initially. A modest increase is more likely to be met. This allows advancement at a later date, when you are more settled in the job, and you have shown your worth.

Some people are frightened that they might 'price themselves out of the market' by asking for salaries which are too high. However, the opposite, asking for a salary which is too low, can indicate a poor level of self-esteem. An employer might wonder why applicants are so desperate as to accept a salary below their value. Have they been turned down so often that they have lowered their sights? And if so, why have they been turned down?

The best tactic is to quote a salary rate slightly above what you need, and to negotiate around that level. In my experience, few employers are likely to penny-pinch if the right applicant comes along.

Do you have any health problems?

I always say that you need only admit to having a health problem if it affects your performance at work, or if there is a strong possibility of it doing so. If you have suffered any illness and it is cured, or you have not suffered an attack for some time, it is best not to mention it. Unless the post requires a medical examination, possible access to your medical files and contact with your General Practitioner, it is wise not to give this kind of information.

What made you apply to our company?

The optimum answer is one which is slightly flattering to the employer, without being patronising. You could quote any information you found out about the employer and their success or, if it is a public sector employer, the value of the service they offer to the community or to the taxpayer. You might mention the career opportunities they can offer, and the size of the organisation. Never reply that you saw their advertisement and just thought that you might apply. Employers will expect to see preparation and research to support your interest in the job.

Have you applied for any other type of job?
In a way it is a bit unfair of an interviewer to ask this
question, but they sometimes do. State that you have
concentrated your job search on this particular type of
vacancy. Don't give the impression that you have applied
for many other types of work. A planned search for this
particular job will demonstrate your motivation and
enthusiasm to the employer and show that you have made
a considered decision to apply.

What kind of equipment have you used?
A fairly simple question – preparation should make it easy
to answer. List any equipment you have used, almost
anything could be included, depending on the job. Office
machinery, photocopiers, switchboard, Word Processors,
Computers; or types of vehicle driven, load size, diesel or
petrol, Fork Lift Truck, electric or diesel, load capacity;
power tools, cash registers, counting machines, production machinery etc. Don't assume that the interviewer is
familiar with the technical terms – he may not be if he is a
personnel officer, or a consultant brought in from outside
the company.

What have you been doing while unemployed?
If you have been out of work for some time then you
should have arranged some kind of activities for yourself.
Voluntary work, odd jobs around the house, training or
study. Make sure that you talk about your job search
activities, and how you have applied to employers on a
speculative basis to show that you are keen to get back
into a job.

   Try to be positive about your unemployment. This
might sound difficult, but if you show that you consider
your period out of work to be temporary (albeit long-
term) it suggests that you have a positive attitude. Try to
give the impression that you know that you will get fixed
up with a job at some point. If you let the employer feel
that you are resigned to unemployment, or that you blame

other people for your predicament, they might think that you would find it difficult to settle back into work.

What can you tell me about the industry?
Your general research should provide enough information for this type of question: the current state of affairs, recent developments, closures, openings, any new legislation. Relevant newspapers and any useful television programmes may give information to quote at an interview.

What kind of person would you say you are?
Use this question to show that you are the kind of person who can do well in the job. Pay attention to the specific requirements of the post and general life skills: ability to communicate, handle responsibility, to share tasks and rewards. Talk about areas of your personality which support your application, but don't say anything negative. Neither should you repeat anything that other people have said: the question is specifically about how *you* see yourself.

These examples are a selection of common interview questions. Preparation will let you handle these and any similar questions efficiently. Read through your CV, think what you have to offer, and work out a few answers in advance.

Second Interviews
Some employers prefer to interview for a second time before making the decision to offer employment. Second interviews vary in their purpose and scope. It can be a more intensive discussion, perhaps with more senior management than the preliminary interview, or it may involve a variety of tests or exercises designed to allow the candidate a wider opportunity to demonstrate his value.
    Sometimes, when two interviews are used, the first is a general discussion, perhaps quite informal, between

employer and applicant. A large number of people may be interviewed. It could be part of an 'open day' to recruit newcomers to the industry or profession. Examples would be Police or Armed Forces Information Fairs, or Graduate Fairs and the Milk Round, which people visit to get information about career opportunities. Arrangements are made for a more detailed interview as part of an organised selection process at a later date, if the candidate chooses to pursue the idea.

A formal two-stage interview system, using a full-scale preliminary interview to select a small number of candidates for a second meeting, is thought to be more objective by many employers. Sequential second interviews, where the second meeting is organised and attended by completely different interviewers, have the advantage that they involve less individual bias than a single interviewer and produce a fairer result. They tend to be used for managerial and professional posts, although some employers use the second interview technique for blue collar jobs as well. If you achieve the distinction of a second interview it means that you impressed your interviewer and are felt worthy of further consideration.

Second interviews often involve participation by company directors or senior level management, and they will use the second interview to verify the points developed in your first meeting. Any topics the personnel manager thought important will have been passed to the directors for further exploration in the second interview.

Preparation for this type of second interview is similar to that for any interview. You have to be ready with good reasons for your application and firm ideas about what you can offer the company and how you would put your skills and experience to use in their organisation. It's no use attending a second interview and repeating the answers from your first meeting. Think of examples of how you used your abilities in previous jobs and what you achieved.

Use the interview to reinforce the idea that you are very

keen to work for them, that your decision to apply was a balanced judgement and that you are interested in staying with them in the long term. The majority of posts involving second interviews are managerial, and the applicant's enthusiasm and length of intended service are very important points. Staff turnover of any kind can cause problems for the employer and management job changes cause particular difficulties. Employers will probe these topics at second interviews.

This second meeting will offer you a better chance to discuss pay, fringe benefits, promotion, the conditions attached to any trial period, or other topics. Having success-fully passed the first selection, you have a stronger footing on which to open a discussion about salary and 'extras'. If the second interview is done by a director, you can talk specifically about pay and conditions. A personnel officer may not have the power to arrange salary and other remunerations for management posts and so the first inter-view might not be a suitable time to raise such matters.

The gap between a first and second interview gives you a breathing space to think of points to raise, or to prepare your answers in more depth. Think carefully about the first interview – were there any questions you expected but which weren't asked? Did you answer everything fully for them? Doing this may give you an idea of the type of questions or topics likely to come up on a second occasion. Gather together any examples of successful performance, improved efficiency, better sales, higher profits etc, for which you were responsible.

The employer will expect to see that you have prepared for the second interview in the same way as you did for the first. Don't assume that everything is cut and dried, make sure you have some fresh material. Keep looking for useful information about the industry or profession, read the relevant journals and newspapers, and be ready to talk about the current situation in the industry.

Occasionally second interview topics are pre-arranged with the applicant. Generally though, employers keep the procedures to themselves, and expect you to anticipate and prepare for their interview.

'Situation' interviews are a popular technique amongst some employers. Here questions relating to the job and everyday events are asked, and the applicant is expected to say what they would do in a given situation: 'What would you do if . . . ?' The Police Force and similar organisations use this system to identify good candidates and it is also used in commerce. It tests your ability to think on your feet and can reveal potential weaknesses in a candidate's attitude and performance.

Tests

Tests are used by employers to assess general attitudes, likely behaviour patterns or specific job skills, i.e. accuracy with figures, observation abilities, communication skills, etc. There are 3 basic types of test:

1 General mental ability
2 Specific occupational aptitude and ability
3 Personality analysis

The first kind assesses verbal, numerical and spatial skills. I.Q. tests are part of this system, and are often used in higher level recruitment. The ability to do abstract reasoning is evaluated in some tests, and questions may involve geometrical shapes, number tests and language assessment. HM Forces and many large commercial organisations use these kinds of tests to select applicants before personality testing to identify optimum job or posting choices.

Tests designed to assess specific occupational ability, or the potential to achieve that ability, include mechanical skills, manual dexterity, information handling, speed typing and computer use. Examples of these kinds of tests include The Crawford Small Parts Test (finger dexterity) and The Purdue Peg Board Test (for eye/hand coordination, such as required in assembly work).

Personality tests examine possible behaviour patterns in particular situations. From the answers, a skilled examiner can draw up a profile of the candidate. The tests use pre-set answer boxes, ranging from extremely good to very poor, with a scale of points in between and the candidate ticks the box which he thinks most accurately indicates his performance or ability. Questions have to be answered quickly with little time to consider the question and bias the result. Indeed, questions are sometimes repeated in a different form to avoid 'cheating'.

This kind of testing is called Psychometric Testing. It can be used in a general sense – to find out what an applicant would be best at doing in an organisation – or to assess if they have the potential to do a specific job. It can be an effective way to select candidates for a second, more in-depth, interview. It is used by employment agencies and many large employers.

The use of psychometric testing makes recruitment fairer and more objective. It cuts out the personal intuition on which traditional interview systems rely. People often ask me how they should deal with psychometric testing, how can they 'slant' their answers? My answer is that you shouldn't try! If the testing is accurate and you are suitable to the post then this will show in your results.

Trying to 'fiddle' your answers will only complicate matters. If the test is used to plan a long-term career for you, then an inaccurate assessment would be very unhelpful. Many employers tend to combine psychometric tests with more normal interview methods, so they are not necessarily a make or break event.

Other types of assessment procedures include applicants talking to a group of people about a topic or performing a task in a set time. Some employers tape record interviews and have the tape examined by a psychologist who specialises in voice analysis. One of the larger breweries employs this technique when interviewing applicants for public house management.

PART SIX

ACCEPTANCE AND REJECTION

What Is An Offer?
When an employer picks the successful candidate, an offer is made. The offer should be written, and should cover all that the parties agreed at the interview. It should include salary payment details, and say to whom you report on the first day. The letter usually includes a return slip confirming that you wish to take up the offer. The start date should take into account the length of notice you are required to give under your present contract.

The offer may be conditional on information you supplied in your application and on reference checking. It is common for your employment to begin with a trial period before full employment is offered, subject to satisfactory performance. You should have discussed the conditions and pay of the trial period at the interview. Trial periods sometimes attract lower pay or less fringe benefits than full employee status. Trial periods can be as long as one year, but a statement of employment, if not a full contract, should be issued within 3 months.

If your offer is not written, then the employer should invite you in to finalise the arrangement and draw up a written statement. It is wise to suggest to the employer that you would prefer a written offer, as it is a better legal basis for employment than just a telephone call. When employers make an offer they generally expect the applicant to accept it, subject to the arrangements being acceptable to both parties. However, strictly speaking, any offer is for you to consider. You might have had an alternative job offered to you, or you may eventually decide to carry on with your present employment.

If there are any points you still wish to discuss or clarify with your prospective employer then this is the time. If the employer has chosen you for the post then you are probably in a strong bargaining position.

If you work in a specialised area, or in a high level post, then the offer is a pivotal point in your negotiations. But don't push your luck! They may have a reserve ready if you don't reply quickly enough, or if you put the ball back in their court by asking for a whole new set of preferential terms of employment. Knowledge of the job market will give you some idea about the value of the package offered to you, and the possibility of pressing for a few more benefits.

If you are unemployed the offer is still conditional. If you refuse the job because the employer imposes a set of unfair working conditions, if you consider their premises or equipment to be unsafe, or for any other valid reason, state benefits will not be affected if you account for your refusal properly to the benefit office. Any trial periods you undertake also need to be accounted for at the benefit office. If you fail to pass the trial or resign from the job of your own choice, the benefit office will want to know why.

A trial period is the length of time which an employer may use to finish his assessment of his new employee. During the trial period the normal rules relating to disciplinary procedures, length of notice etc., do not apply. Both parties may finish their side of the agreement without notice. You have to deal with a trial period carefully because as a new employee you are under observation and assessment. If you like, you can consider it as a type of extended interview, in which your attitude and performance are being assessed in practical situations. You must make sure that your attitude and activities during the trial period support your application.

Your new employer will be anxious to make sure that you match the impression you gave him at your formal interview and that you really can do the job. An offer of employment does not automatically mean that you will receive full contract status (with legal protection). In most jobs you have to earn employee status through the trial period.

Contracts

Within 13 weeks of taking up your post your employer should issue you with a written contract under the provisions of the Employment Protection Acts.

Specifically the contract should identify the following items:

The parties to the contract
The start date of employment
Pay and conditions, holiday entitlement, sickness and injury arrangements
Notice entitlement to both parties
Job title and duties
Disciplinary and grievance procedures
Fringe benefits, pensions etc.

Some employers supplement this with a Job Description giving more specific details about the post and the duties.

Starting Your New Post

A new job or a return to employment brings new challenges, new people to meet and deal with, new procedures, new equipment, a new hierarchy to fit into, a new journey to and from work and many other changes. It is important that once you have got your new job you start off on the right footing with your new employer. Remember, especially if you are on a trial period, that you will be under observation: it is your employer's first opportunity to assess you in practical situations.

Here are some ideas for the trial period.

1 Maintain good punctuality.
2 Look alert and interested, show enthusiasm for the post.
3 Get to know other people – don't miss any chance to mix with your new workmates or colleagues.
4 Watch your sense of humour! Your joke may be another's insult.
5 A new job makes you tired – you're under a lot of pressure to learn new names and to stay on top – so cut down on social activities or sports for a few weeks.
6 Don't follow other employees' bad habits – they may have worked at the company for a long time and are able to cut corners. You can't!
7 Accept advice from other employees, even if you know how to do the job. (If you get a reputation for being a know-all, then, when you do need help, no-one may be willing to assist.)
8 Always ask if you're not sure of the correct procedure.
9 Get to know the layout of the premises quickly, spot possible danger areas, fire exits, dangerous machinery etc.
10 Follow rules, respect other people and the employer's property and premises.

Matters to consider when starting a new post.

1 Do you need a bank or a building society account to receive wages? If you need to open a new account then shop around and check out the types of account which are open – some current accounts pay interest, or offer other incentives. Generally building societies take a little longer to clear payments than banks.
2 Your new employer will require your national insurance number, and evidence of your last tax code (normally

shown on your P45, in the UK, which should be sent by the benefit office soon after you commence work).

3 How long will it be before your first pay day? Some organisations take a while to process new employees' details. Others may make a special first payday arrangement for new members of staff, and then normal systems are followed from the second pay day onwards. If you think you are going to have problems waiting for your first salary payment then ask your new employer to consider a 'sub'.

If you are unemployed, this is even more important. If you sign off the benefit system and there is a gap between your last giro cheque and the first pay day, you might have problems. Sometimes loans from the Department of Social Security are available to help bridge this gap. Make sure that you arrange these if you will need one to pay for meals, travel expenses and household bills.

GOOD LUCK!

Better Luck Next Time
Everyone must be prepared for possible rejection. Try not to be too disappointed. The successful candidate will have had some slight edge on everyone else. Being rejected does not necessarily mean that you are bad at interviews, and if you persist with your applications then ultimately you should succeed.

If you are prepared to analyse your unsuccessful interviews you will learn valuable lessons. For interview skills, experience is the best teacher. After you have been to an interview, don't mentally sweep it under the carpet. Think about it. Did it go well? Were there any questions you felt were awkward or difficult to answer? Did you answer all their questions fully? Did you prepare sufficiently beforehand? Did you plan your route to the interview properly? By checking through these points, perhaps making notes about how you felt it went, you can identify any weak areas in your interviews. Keep an interview diary, with notes about your previous meetings with employers. Fill it in soon after the interview, when it is still fresh in your memory. Later you can refer to it and see the areas which you need to work on. If you failed a test, practise it at home, then the next time you meet one you will be better prepared.

You could also contact the employer to talk about your application. Enquire if you made any errors which let you down; could they give you any positive criticism to help you identify problems in your interviews? Some employers will help in this way if you ask politely and make it obvious that you are not complaining about your interview result.

Another way to improve your interview technique is to 'role play' the interview situation with a friend playing the part of an employer, running through the interview procedure, and then assessing your performance. Some recruitment and careers guidance services offer this service for a fee.

Resist the temptation to forget your interview because you failed. Careful assessment of your performance in the interview situation can strengthen your hand for future applications.

Conclusion
If you follow this book then you will increase your chances of success in getting a job. The main thing is to keep up the hunt for a new job despite any rejections you may receive. Determination and the will to succeed are what separates the achievers from the non-achievers.

Keep organised. Don't fall into the trap of sloppy organisation. Keep records of your activities, constantly monitor all avenues of opportunity and vacancies, and keep abreast of developments in your type of work.

Everyone can improve their application skills: as a Job Club leader I have worked with highly educated professional people who thought they knew how to apply for jobs. Having completed my training course they realised that they had been handling applications badly, and their results reflected this. It makes no difference what your background or qualifications are: if you make poor applications you will not succeed.

Be positive. Keep alert and fit. Keep the applications going, and your turn will come. You will win your new job!

GOOD HUNTING!

PART SEVEN

APPENDIX

Useful sources of help or information

Careers Advice

Careers Consultants	Commercial services offering career change advice, testing and interview training.
Careers Services	Advice and counselling on job choice.
Disablement Registration Officer	Job Centre staff who consider applications for disabled status and access to special initiatives.
NACRO	Help and support for ex-offenders, training and job search assistance.

Companies (information on)

Business Libraries	Information on large companies, size, assets and main areas of activity.

Financial Matters

Career Development Loans	Available to unemployed people to finance courses.
Claimant Advisor	Benefits office staff who give advice and information relating to the benefit system.
The Benefits Agency	Help and assistance with Social Security, benefits and National Insurance contributions.

Travel to Interview Scheme	Job Centre facility to pay for journeys to and from interviews for unemployed applicants.

General

Citizens' Advice Bureau	General advice for members of the public.
Job Club	Provider of free resources and job search training for unemployed people

Training

Customised Employment Training	Course of vocational training of short duration and with a definite post at the end of training.
Employment Training	Course of vocational training, usually leading to certificated levels.
Further Education Colleges	Part- and full-time courses in various subjects.
Training Enterprise Councils	Providers of vocational training for unemployed people

Vacancies/Recruitment

Employment Agencies	Commercial recruitment companies.
Employment Services	Vacancies, information and services for job seekers.
Job Interview Guarantee Scheme	Job Centre staff who handle vacancies and market people to local employers.
National Press	Vacancies and information.
Regional/Local Press	As above.
Trade/Professional Journals	Specific trade information and advertisements.

Voluntary Work

Employment Action	Volunteer work for unemployed people and some assistance with job search
Volunteer Bureaux	Organisers of local voluntary work.

INDEX